PRAISE FOR
SPORT PSYCHOLOGY FOR CYCLISTS

"I like the book! Especially the real-life examples and observations. Anyone who reads this book and takes the time to fully embrace each concept will become a better athlete and person."
—Ray Cipollini, directeur sportif of Navigators professional cycling team

"An excellent book for the novice to the pro. Everyone will get something out of it. It has helped me grow and relearn some important aspects I had neglected. In short, the wolf has been found!"
—Brian Walton, Team Saturn

"It's very helpful. If you use it as a workbook and actually do the homework, then I think you will find it really, really beneficial."
—Chrissy Redden, Team Ritchie

"Sport Psychology for Cyclists describes the hows and whys of mental training to become better cyclists. It's a must-read for all our riders and coaches."
—Pierre Hutsebaut, director of Canada's national team programs

SPORT PSYCHOLOGY
FOR CYCLISTS

*by Dr. Saul Miller
and Peggy Maass Hill*

VELO
press

BOULDER, COLORADO USA

International Standard Book Number: 1-884737-68-4

Library of Congress Cataloging-in-Publication Data:

Miller, Saul (Saul B.)
    Sport psychology for cyclists / by Saul Miller and Peggy Maass Hill.
       p. cm. — (The ultimate training series from VeloPress)
    Includes bibliographical references (p.) and index.
    ISBN 1-884737-68-4 (pbk.)
    1. Cycling—Psychological aspects. 2. Cycling—Training.
I. Hill, Peggy Maass, 1959- . II. Title. III. Series
GV1043.7,M55 1999   99-37808
796.6'01'9—dc21   CIP

PRINTED IN THE USA

Distributed in the United States and Canada by Publishers Group West.

VELO *press*

1830 N. 55th Street • Boulder, Colorado • 80301-2700 • USA
303/440-0601 • FAX 303/444-6788 • E-MAIL velopress@7dogs.com

To purchase additional copies of this book or other Velo products,
call 800/234-8356 or visit us on the Web at www.velogear.com

Cover Design: Erin Johnson
Interior layout/production: Paula Megenhardt
Editor: Lori Hobkirk

ACKNOWLEDGMENTS

We wish to express our gratitude to the following individuals who contributed to the creation of this book: to Amy Sorrells, Lori Hobkirk, and their colleagues at VeloPress for making the book something special; to Donald Maass for generously taking time to shepherd us to a suitable agreement; to Brian Walton, Ray Cipollini, Chrissy Redden, Dr. Gloria Cohen, Pierre Hutsebaut and Eric Wohlberg, who read parts of the manuscript and provided excellent constructive feedback; to Marshall Cant, Trevor Cooper, Walter Lai, Robert Major, Susan Kerr, and OBR photography for permission to use their photographs in the book; to the Coaching Association of Canada for allowing us to use a skills development list from the Canadian National Coaching Certification Program Level One Theory Manual, and the Canadian Cycling Association for permission to use the Cycling High Performance Athlete Profile chart; and to John Hill and Laara Maxwell for providing the authors with concerned support.

We would also like to acknowledge some of the riders, coaches and sport professionals who we had the pleasure to learn from and work with over the years. The riders are: Peg's teammates on Rutgers University Intercollegiate Cycling Team, Team Bogus, North Jersey Bike Club, International Christian Cycling Club, Kreb's Cycle Club; and trade teammates Betsy Davis, Beth Heiden, Kelly Kitteredge, Cindy Olavarri, Rebecca Twigg (all from Team 7-Eleven); Marianne Berglund, Rebecca Daughton, Bunki Bankaitis-Davis, Sue

Ehlers, Susie Simpson (Centurion cycling team); Carol Addy, Lisa Brambani, Liz Chapman, Renee Duprell, Sue Sutton, Amy Gibson, Phyllis Hines, Laura Gnagey, Sara Neil, Laura Peycke, Annie Serotniak, Sally Zack (Weight-Watchers team); and all the team managers, soigneurs and mechanics, especially Mark White and Glen Copus. Thanks to all the race directors; officials; and coaches Andrzej Bek, Eddie "B" Borysewicz, Verna Buhler, Patty Cashman, Paul Deem, Des Dickie, Len Goodman, Ron Hayman, John Hill, Pierre Hutsebaut, Jenny John, Yury Kachirin, Tim Kelly, Barry "Bas" Lycett, Oliver "Butch" Martin, Sue Reber, the late Mary Jane Reoch, Barry Shepley and the late Mike Walden. Sport professionals Dr. Barbara Berkowitz, Dr. Susan Butt, Dr. Gloria Cohen, Dr. Emily Goetz, Dr. Andy Jacobs, Dr. Bruce Ogilvie, Dr. Jack Taunton, and the staffs at the U.S. Olympic Training Center and the Canadian Cycling Association. Thanks also to bike sponsors Centurion, Kona, Trek, Raleigh, Rocky Mountain, Serotta and long-time supporters Andiamo! and PowerBar. Plus the following riders, Marie Claude Audet, Steve Bauer, Paul Blanchette, Keith Bruneau, Genny Brunet, Verna Buhler, Francie Crowley, Cindy Devine, Tanya Dubnicoff, Louis Garneau, Scott Goguen, Curt Harnett, Pierre Harvey, Damian O'Hagen, Andreas Hestler, Linda Jackson, Charlie Ko, Chris Koberstein, Jacques Landry, Cory LeClerc, Gary Longhi, Melanie McQuaid, Darnelle Moore, Lori-Ann Muenzer, Jay Petersen, Gervais Rioux, David Spears, Andrew Shandro, Bruce Spicer, Alex Steida, Karen Strong, Lesley Tomlinson, Alison Sydor, Debra Tamblyn, Yvon Waddell, Brian Walton, Marilyn Wells, Martin Willock, Eric Wohlberg, Tony Zarsadias, Laurel Zilke and Adrianne Zonta. (Peg gives a special thanks to everyone she has raced with from 1982 to the present.)

Lastly, Peg wants to thank her family who supported her racing career: Margery, Don, Donald, Tim and Gretchen.

DEDICATION

To those cyclists who keep the rubber side down.

TABLE OF CONTENTS

PREFACE

Cycling is a mirror and a path to self discovery. It can be a demanding, enjoyable sport. Demanding because it can challenge the rider to give everything, and the challenge is a psycho-physical one. Cycling can be physically and mentally exhausting. It can also be a stimulating and relaxing experience. In that respect it is truly recreational. When you ride you get energy. You are re-created.

Cycling is a world sport. All over the planet people ride and race bicycles. They race them along highways, along country roads and city streets, up and down mountain trails, through forests, and around steeply banked velodromes. Everywhere the riders confront their fears, the clock, the elements, themselves, and each other in their quest to go faster.

The more we work with bicycle riders and racers, the clearer it becomes that cycling is an individual sport and that there are wide differences in what cyclists do to mentally prepare and to perform at their best. These differences are a function of the individual make-up of the rider—who they are—and the nature of their event—the kind of race they ride. In *Sport Psychology for Cyclists* we describe the basics of how to manage your mind so that you can perform at your best in any cycling situation.

INTRODUCTION

My name is Dr. Saul Miller. I am a sport psychologist. Peg Maass Hill and I are pleased to provide a sport psychology program for cyclists that we hope will help you to be more successful in your cycling and experience more satisfaction from the sport. Specifically, it will help you to have a better understanding of the psychological aspect of cycling, and experience more ease and power and a more productive focus.

The training camp

In presenting this information to you we have done it in a session format. An experienced cycling coach, Peg, has arranged for eight riders—a mix of men and women, roadies, trackies, and mountain bikers—to experience a number of sessions with a sport psychologist who has been working with cyclists for years. There are eight sessions in all. Throughout the "training camp" we provide specific information for road riders, mountain bikers, downhillers and track racers, as well as people who are simply interested recreational riders.

The fundamentals we wanted to cover in the eight sessions were the feelings, focus, attitudes, competence and

1

individual differences we all experience while we ride a bike. In discussing feelings, we wanted to describe how to use breathing, relaxation and arousal techniques to enhance emotional control. The sessions on focus explore how to use thoughts and images to enhance performance. The session on an optimal cycling attitude discusses commitment, confidence, identity and deserving. In the session on competence we integrate physical and mental training with developing the specific technical skill sets required by each cycling speciality, and then relating that to confidence. Then, it was important to include a session on individual differences to illustrate how people are different from each other and how understanding your style can help you to train, prepare and perform more effectively.

Initially, we were not clear which of these topics we should present first. Since more people relate sport psychology to visualization, imagery, self talk and attitude, we thought it might be easier to introduce those ideas at the start of the book. However, in the end, we decided to write the book just as Dr. Miller would actually do the training—by focusing on feelings first. That meant introducing breathing, relaxation and arousal techniques in the first two sessions. Normally, after listening to an athlete describe his or her situation, consultation begins by helping the athlete to relax and generate "good feelings." As people learn to regulate their feelings, usually by using breathing, the quality and clarity of their thoughts and images improves. They feel stronger; their goals, self-talk and images are more positive, and they seem more confident. The bottom line is they are more responsive to the rest of the training.

We have written the book in the first person. When I speak, I usually talk in the first person as "I." When Peg and I are both making comments it's presented as "we." And when Peg speaks the return to regular text is noted with a dropped capital letter.

Before we begin I want to ask, "Why do you cycle?"

Think about it. What are your cycling goals? What do you aspire to? If you are a competitive cyclist, why do you race or ride?

Your reasons for cycling shape your goals, and goals provide the direction and juice to get you where you want to go.

As a cyclist, what are your long term goals?

What are your cycling goals for the next five years?

What are your goals for this season?

Your goals affect your plan and process. What are your goals for the month? For this week? For today's race or ride?

In this training camp we have defined a goal for each of the eight sessions. It's an aid to keep in

ROBERT MAJOR

"The most powerful thing you can do is set goals. The most important thing is the mind. That's where the power is, believing in your goals."

– Alison Sydor

3

mind as you work with the training elements and exercises that follow.

If the reason you race and ride is to be as good as you can be and to excel at the psycho-physical challenge that cycling presents, then it's important to explore the mental aspects of the sport. This training camp will do that. It will enhance your understanding and competence of the mental game and it will help you be an optimal cyclist.

"Feel it. See it. Believe it. Do it."
—Dr. Miller

Managing
mind and
emotions

"The real race is not on the hot, paved roads, the torturous off-road course or the smooth-surfaced velodrome. It is in the electrochemical pathways of your mind."
—Alexi Grewal, Olympic gold medalist[1]

T he goal of the first chapter is to highlight the importance of mental training and to introduce breathing as a basic way to manage emotions.

Success in cycling and success in life is learning how to manage your mind.

Most athletes and coaches would agree that success in their sport is at least 50 percent "mental" and the result of the mind and body working well together. Indeed, excellence in any sport is the result of the successful integration of physical, technical and mental factors. However, in reality this idea of integration of mind and body is under-practiced in preparing athletes for most sports, and there is a disproportional focus on the physical and technical aspects of training. Mental training is relatively ignored.

[1] "The Quotable Cyclist," edited by Bill Stickland, Breakaway Books, New York, 1997.

It's the same in cycling.

In our first chapter we will go over some general principles about how to manage the mind more effectively. As a talented athlete with a genuine interest in cycling, you want to increase your cycling enjoyment and success. To do that it's beneficial to explore the mental side of the sport. Let's begin.

The way I see it, the mind is like a television set....

Your mental TV is always on.
If what you are watching
doesn't feel good to you,
or if it doesn't give you power,
change the channel.
It's your TV.
You're the boss.
You are response-able.

Most of the cyclists we work with are healthy people with sound, high-functioning minds. As such, they are response-able to run positive, empowering programs on their mental TVs.

My job as a sport psychologist is to show you ways to change channels on the TV, and to help you to develop better quality programs to tune into. Indeed, that's what *Sport Psychology for Cyclists* is about.

There are three key operating principles for managing your mind effectively.

1. The first idea or principle is that the mind is like a TV set. You control the switch on that mental TV. You are in charge.

If what you're watching doesn't give you power or pleasure, change the channel.

Staying tuned-in to the power channel is a matter of choice.

2. You get more of what you think about. If what you put on your mental TV causes you to feel tense, anxious or depressed, then staying tuned in to those thoughts and feelings will generate a greater sense of negativity and disease—and gives you more things to worry about in your life.

In contrast, if what you focus on is something that inspires you and gives you energy, you are more likely to create success and enjoyment in life. So, it's important that we tune into positive "power" programs on the TV.

Sounds simple enough. Then, you may ask "Why don't we simply create positive thoughts and feelings all the time?"

3. The third principle relates to the way we're "hard-wired" as human beings. The way our nervous systems work is that our feelings affect our thoughts, and our thoughts affect our feelings. Every time you have a feeling, automatically a thought goes with it.

I used to run a pain clinic treating people who had been injured and were living with chronic pain. If someone had a pain in their back, automatically a thought would pop into their mind. The thought could be "Ow, I hurt," or "There's something wrong with me," "I need some medication," or

"I'd better lie down." The specific thought didn't matter; the important point to understand is that whenever there was a painful feeling, automatically a cautious thought went with it. It's the way we're wired.

Similarly, our thoughts automatically affect our feelings.

Sometimes we create circular—thought-feeling—loops that limit us.

The feelings that most frequently affect and limit cyclists are fear, pain and difficulty. The latter may take the form of not having the energy to challenge or persevere, or feeling a sense of impossibility in relation to the difficult task at hand.

The problem is, these kinds of negative feelings can produce "limited thinking," and limited or negative thinking can, in turn, feed back into feelings creating a negative loop that is like a trap. That's exactly what a "slump" is; negative feelings feed and produce negative thoughts that create and produce more negative feelings.

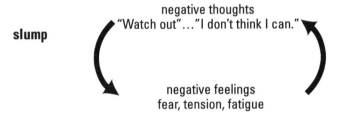

slump

negative thoughts
"Watch out"..."I don't think I can."

negative feelings
fear, tension, fatigue

Brain balance: Excellence is a product of an integration of mind and body. It is facilitated by having "brain balance," a smooth, integrated, functioning of the left and right halves of the cerebral cortex of the brain.

Research has indicated that our brains consist of two cerebral hemispheres and that each hemisphere processes a different quality of information. The left brain processes logical, analytic and technical information. It is verbal and it's about thought, reason, detail, planning (future) and analysis (past).

The right brain provides an intuitive and synthesizing function. It is nonverbal and deals more with feelings and images. It is spontaneous and focused on the present.

left hemisphere		right hemisphere
thinking		feeling
analytic		intuitive
planning		spontaneous
past/future		present
words		images

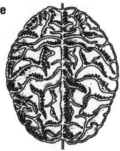

Optimal cycling is a result of a smooth and integrated functioning between left and right cerebral hemispheres, between mind and body, and between feeling and focus. Breathing is a key to integrating these functions.[2]

BREATHE

Winning is more than thinking positive. One of the basics to success is learning how to have emotional control. Stated simply, if you can't manage your emotions, you won't control your performance and you won't perform at your best. The best and easiest way to develop emotional control is to focus on your breathing.

Breathing is a process that integrates mind and body. As we focus on our breath we bring our consciousness more into the here and now. Experiencing a smooth breathing rhythm primes and integrates brain function. From a performance perspec-

[2] Also see homework assignment No. 5.

tive, relaxed and rhythmical breathing enhances our image of what we are capable of being; it increases our motivation and supports us in realizing our goals.

Breathing is fundamental in our lives.

Breathing is a key to power and self-control.

Breathing awareness is especially important for cyclists who experience oxygen debt, stretch the psycho-physical limits to the maximum, and often perform under intense pressure.

EXERCISE NO. 1:
BREATHING AND GENERATING POSITIVE FEELINGS

To begin training, I'd like to show you a simple breathing exercise that is basic to emotional control. Please sit or lie back.

I am going to ask you to tune into three things in your breathing.

Rhythm

The most important part of breathing is the rhythm of your breath.

Simply feel the breath come in...
and feel the breath go out....

Again, feel the breath come in...
and feel the breath go out....

Spend a minute or two just watching the breath
come in...and go out.

The key to rhythm is time.
Give yourself time for the in breath to come in…all the way in….
Give yourself time for the out breath to flow out…
all the way out.

The breath is like waves in the ocean.
And the waves never rush.

Sit back, relax, give yourself time to
feel the in breath flowing in.
Give yourself time to feel the out breath flowing out.
It's very simple. There's power in simplicity.

Inspiration

Once you have tuned into your breathing rhythm, the second thing to focus on is the in-breath—the inspiration.

If breathing is respiration, then the in-breath is inspiration.
Inspiration means to take in spirit.
Your breathing is a source of energy and spirit.

Again, tune into your breathing.
Experience a nice smooth rhythm.
Give yourself time.

As you breathe, place a little more emphasis on the in breath.
Draw in energy with each breath you take.
You have a personal connection to an unlimited supply.

On the out breath allow yourself to release.
Let go of used energy and negativity.

Again, feel yourself gently pulling in energy with each in breath.
On the out breath, simply allow yourself to release and relax.

USING BREATHING IS THE KEY
TO MANAGING EMOTIONS.

WALTER LAI DESIGNS

Some cyclists have found it useful when they ride to think of breathing in fresh, charged energy— and breathing out used energy and lactic acid.

DIRECTION

Experience a nice smooth rhythm and feel yourself breathing in energy. Now, focus on directing that energy. Allow yourself to imagine sending that energy down through your hips and glutes and quads, down into your calves and right into the soles of your feet.

Again, allow yourself to imagine breathing in energy and sending, allowing, directing that energy down through the hips and legs, into the feet—into the power pads in the soles of the feet—and right into the pedals of the bike.

Again, feel yourself drawing in energy.

Now imagine that you are directing or sending that energy through your shoulders and out through your arms into your hands.

Allow the energy to flow right into the palms of your hands.

Again, imagine yourself drawing in energy and allow or direct the flow of that energy through your shoulders and arms and into the palms of your hands, right into the handlebars of the bike.

Feel yourself breathing in energy.

This time imagine sending energy up, along the spinal column up through the neck into the head, into the eyes.

Experience a smooth breathing rhythm, draw in energy again, imagine energy flowing up the spinal column, up through the neck, up into the head and eyes so that you can see clearly, with great peripheral vision.

EXERCISE No. 2: THE FIVE-POINTED STAR

Experience a smooth breathing rhythm.

Feel yourself drawing in energy and send it down through the quads and calves into the feet…
out through the shoulders, arms, into the hands…
up the spinal column into the head and the eyes like a five-pointed star.

It's important to pair your feelings with your thoughts.
As you direct the energy out, say to yourself, "I am a star."

Breathe smoothly.
Draw energy in.
Send it out like a star.
Think and feel "I am a star."
Good.

EXERCISE NO. 3: TENSION RELEASE

The next part of managing feelings has to do with being better able to release tension.

Tension is heavy. Tension can be an exhausting and limiting drag.

Sit back, relax and breathe.
Experience how your body feels.
Experience the contrasting feelings of tension and release.

Hands

In order to experience those contrasting feelings, create some tension in your hands by making fists. As you do, feel the tension in the central part of the hand and the fingers. Now, turn your wrists in so you feel an additional tension in the back of your hands.

Squeeze your fists. Hold it (four to five seconds).
Feel the tension. Now let it go. Just let it drop.
Release...
and after you release, take a breath.

What you want to experience and practice is the feeling of release and breathe.

People rarely hold a lot of tension in their hands unless

they are angry. However, hands are an excellent place to begin exploring the tension-release process, since people are very aware of them.

Shoulders

Next, focus your attention on your shoulders. Raise you shoulders up two or three inches. Hold it, and feel the tension there. The neck and shoulders are a primary tension holding area.

Let go.

Release and breathe.

It's always, release and breathe. But this time raise your shoulders up one-half inch. It's hardly noticeable, but you can feel it. Notice as you do that you cut down your breathing. And breath is power.

Now release your shoulders. After you do, take a breath.

From time to time, cue your body for tension. And always remember to release and breathe.

It's always release and breathe.

Chest and abdomen

As you relax and breathe, place a hand on your chest and one hand on your abdomen. Now simply sit or lie back and feel these parts of your body expand and contract with each breath that you take.

The breath is like waves in the ocean.

Feel the waves rise and fall with each breath you take.

Allow your chest and abdomen to be free to expand and contract with each breath you take.

Pubic area

Now focus your attention on the genitals. Squeeze that sphincter muscle that you tighten when you hold back in not going to the toilet...or during sex. Squeeze that muscle and notice how that even calms down your breathing.

Hold it four to five seconds, then release and take a breath.
It's always release and breathe.

You can tense or release any part of your body.

You're the boss. You're in control. What's important is that you learn how to scan the body, feel where you have tension and let it go. Then go back to the power source which is breathing.

The release reflex involves awareness, release and breathing. It's the key to releasing unnecessary tension and having more emotional control.

Feet

Finally, curl your toes, making fists with your feet.
As you do so, experience the tension in your feet.
It's like a bird gripping a perch.
Feel the tension and hold it four to five seconds.
Now let it go.
Release and take a breath.
Remember, whenever you feel tension, always release and breathe.

Now let's review the relaxation experience.
To begin, notice the rhythm of your breath.
The key to rhythm is time.
Give yourself time for that breath to come all the way in.

Place one hand on your chest and the other on your abdomen.
Feel the in breath come all the way in....
Feel the out breath flowing all the way out.

As you breathe, place a little more emphasis on the in breath.
With each in breath feel yourself drawing in energy....
Send or allow that energy to flow down through the legs and
the feet.
Send or allow that energy to flow out through the arms and
the hands.
Send or allow that energy to flow up the spinal
column through the neck, into the head and the eyes.

Allow yourself to feel powerful.
Allow yourself to be a star.

Good.

Are there any questions?

One rider asks a question that several of
the riders have been thinking:

QUESTION: This feels relaxing enough, but frankly I don't see
how it's going to help me when I'm exhausted and I have
another hill to climb, or a sprint, or when I want to go faster.
What does this relaxed breathing stuff have to do with competitive racing?

DR. MILLER A good question. As we said earlier, success in
bicycle racing...and in life is about learning how to manage

your mind. A key to managing your mind is being able to generate feelings of calm and power in any situation. Then, it's about focusing your energies on what you want to do.

PEG Let me give you an example. In mountain-bike racing, riders often crash just after completing a difficult section of the course, whether it's a hard climb or a technical single-track section. They have just worked very hard and they are tired. It's as if they let up and lost focus and control after they have survived the short-term challenge. If they would simply focus on maintaining a smooth breathing rhythm they would be better able to stay focused and in control—and these "let down" accidents would be less likely to happen. Likewise, you can use your breathing paired with power thoughts to prepare for the next climb, calling on more energy and power.

Another example of how to use breathing is when you need to slow down in order to make good choices. What if you get to a race and discover you have left some essential piece of equipment, such as your shoes, at home? By relaxing and taking a breath instead of panicking, you may be better able to come up with some intelligent action choices such as finding a suitable borrowing source, locating the nearest available bike shop, going back and getting the shoes, or taping your feet to the pedals. As a coach, I have been faced with all of these choices and being calm has helped to deal with these and similar challenges effectively.

A world-class mountain biker related how this happened to her at a World Cup event. She was getting ready to start the race and realized that she had left her racing numbers in the condo where she was staying. Her team mechanic knew she was staying nearby and ran off to get the numbers. However, the seconds were ticking away. With less than five minutes to go she was at the start line. With less than one minute to go she lined up at the start, and the mechanic was pinning on her numbers. She rode an excellent race. Afterward she said what helped her keep it together was the mechanic—and remembering to breathe smoothly.

In this chapter we have been describing a simple, effective technique for creating feelings of calm and power. As you breathe smoothly and rhythmically you will use your energy more effectively, feel lighter and have less fatigue—and you will be better able to control your feelings.

EXERCISE NO. 4: IMAGING AND BREATHING

All right, let's go through it again, and this time let's relate it to cycling. Relax and breathe. As you do, feel yourself drawing in energy.

Experience energy flowing through you—like a star.

Now, allow yourself to imagine that you are on your bicycle.

Imagine that you are riding with smoothness and power.

You have good form.

You are drawing in energy.

Energy is flowing through you.

You have strength through the glutes and quads.

You are spinning, the cranks, or turning over the pedals with ease.

Your upper body is relaxed.

You are feeling good.

Imagine you can feel energy flowing up the spinal column, flowing up into clear eyes—you can see clearly.

You are breathing easy, you are riding with ease and power.

You have great form and are feeling good.

If you see that you're holding tension, don't drag it around with you. Let it go.

Draw in energy.

Experience energy flowing through the body.

Think about yourself as a star.

And imagine riding with smoothness and power.

Enjoyment is the foundation of the whole optimal cycling process. One of the keys to being a successful cyclist is to enjoy riding your bicycle. It's your response-ability to create feelings of ease and power—and to channel your energy into technique and form on the bicycle.

EMPOWERMENT

Empowerment is a popular word these days. To my mind the beginning of being empowered is tuning into your breathing and drawing in energy. Then sending or allowing that energy to flow through your total being.

Gail came to see me prior to her road race at an important international Games. It was late in her season, which included success in the grueling *Tour de France Féminin*. When I met her she was tired, and after a long 20-hour flight she didn't feel much like racing in the hot humid weather of the tropics. To make matters worse, along with jet lag and fatigue, she had strained a muscle in a training ride and she was hurting. Since feelings affect thinking, it's not surprising that Gail's fatigue and dis-ease were contributing to her thinking less-than-positive thoughts.

I listened to her describe her feelings for a few minutes, then we began to work with her breathing—with rhythm and inspiration. In a few minutes she began to feel more comfortable and more powerful. As she felt more powerful her confidence grew. We had two sessions before the road race. Gail rode a good race finishing at the head of the field and supporting her teammate who won the gold medal.

Forty-eight hours after the road race was another grueling challenge, the time trial. Again, the feelings of fatigue and dis-ease began to play and reduce Gail's power and confidence. And again, we spent several sessions focusing Gail on her breathing, on rhythm, inspiration and streaming energy out like a star. As she did, she began to feel "empowered." Then, we added some positive race imagery to the good feelings, and Gail was ready to go. And go she did, winning a silver medal at the Games.

Just as this world class racer used breathing to empower herself, and the rider at the start line used breathing to calm down, anyone affected by the stresses of daily life can use breathing to recharge and prepare for a challenging ride. Indeed, many of the examples in this training program are of competitive and elite cyclists because they frequently perform under intense pressure. However, the technology that we're describing is simple and useful for everyone.

Power is a force that will work for you.

Breathing is the key to filling yourself with energy and power.

Tap the mains.

Draw in energy.

Let energy flow through you.

That's the focus of our first chapter.

HOMEWORK

There are five homework assignments. I strongly encourage you to be diligent about your practice of these assignments.

1. The first assignment is to work with breathing. (Exercises No. 1-2)

Create a 10-minute breathing session every day in which you sit or lie back, get into your breathing, experience a smooth breathing rhythm—the waves flow in and the waves flow out. As you experience rhythm, emphasize the in breath, drawing in energy. Then feel that energy flowing out through the body, like a five-pointed star.

2. After relaxing and breathing for about six or seven minutes, for just a minute or two imagine yourself riding with smoothness, power and ease. Imagine that you are riding in slow motion. Imagine turning the wheels smoothly and easily, and that you are riding with power, speed and excellent form. (Exercise No.4)

Experience 10 minutes of relaxed breathing at least once a day with some smooth-riding imagery. Two sessions a day would be even better.

3. As you ride your bicycle consciously experience yourself breathing in energy, and feel the energy flow through you
as you ride. Speed up breathing for 10 breaths. Just watch 10
breaths flow in, and flow out, especially through the legs and
feet, and up through the spinal column into the head and
eyes—a five-pointed star—flowing in and flowing out. Experience at least three or four 10-breath cycles on each ride.

The first chapter is about creating positive feelings that
we will use to generate an optimal cycling mind set. With
mental training, what you put in is what you'll get out. It's
the same as with physical training.

4. The fourth assignment is one that begins in the first
chapter and lasts for the entire eight chapters. We would like
everyone to keep a journal, a record of their mental training
process.

Write down what you did each day and each week, along
with any significant comments and observations. We have
provided several samples of journal writing to illustrate training progressions, pre-race patterns and post-race analysis and
feedback in Appendix A. Read through these entries and
experiment with how recording your thoughts and feelings
about your cycling on a regular basis can positively impact
your cycling experience. Be honest with yourself.

5. For something a little more far out here's a brain-bal-
ancing exercise that you may want to try. It involves drawing
a large—3-foot-wide by 1-foot-high—lemniscate (a horizon-
tal figure-eight) on a piece of paper and putting it on a wall
6 feet in front of you. Then trace the line of the lemniscate
with your finger or your eyes. Try this exercise, two five-

minute sessions for 10 days. Observe if it has any positive impact on your perception or feelings.

HOMEWORK REVIEW

The homework gives some reality to the training sessions. It's important that you take these suggestions and work with them between chapters, and then review your experiences so that you can adapt, adjust and evolve an effective training process. If you don't work the training suggestions, you won't be able to know how effective the process is for you.

As I said before, if questions arise during your training, discuss them with your coach or a knowledgeable cycling partner.

FROM THE GROUP OF EIGHT RIDERS AT THE TRAINING SESSIONS:

ATHLETE I like thinking of myself as a steam engine on the single-track, so the breathing worked as if it were the white steam blasting out of the smoke stack. I used the sound of the train for rhythm, which is slow but powerful.

PEG That's an excellent use of imagery. It doesn't matter if everyone knows tactics like that. It has to be used to be successful.

ATHLETE This is different for me. I am usually very visual, but this homework focused on feeling the breathing and rhythm, and I brought in the ocean sound you suggested, the continuous waves. It was very relaxing and it made me feel peaceful.

PEG Good, that can help you relax and focus before events.

ATHLETE In a team pursuit, things can get pretty panicky, especially getting back on, so focusing on breathing helped me to be calmer and steadier. It also helped me to lower my heart rate and prepare me for the next push.

PEG That's a good observation. It applies to every situation. You can always use your breathing to calm down and take a look at the bigger picture.

Before the event, if you are nervous and if you notice shallow, rapid breathing, remind yourself to calm down. Adjust your breathing. It will help you to replace anxious thoughts with more positive task-oriented confidence builders.

ATHLETE I fell asleep doing the breathing and visualizing, and I keep thinking about food. What am I doing wrong?

PEG When working on any skill, it's best to take care of primary needs first. So if you are hungry, eat and rehydrate; if you're tired, take a nap. If this problem persists, you might think of working with your breathing at some point in the day when you are more alert.

ATHLETE Are you supposed to breathe out of your mouth or your nose?

PEG Habit and level of effort will dictate whether you inhale through your nose or mouth. Generally, it's advisable to breathe through the nose. It is a more developed piece of respiratory equipment with better capabilities to warm and filter the air you breathe in. You can also control the pace of your breath by slowing down the exhale to lower heart rate and relax muscles. Work with it. Mastering your breathing will give you the sense of slowing time.

ATHLETE I thought that tracing the figure eight was cool. I don't know what it does for my cycling, but I thought it was relaxing.

SAUL If something makes sense to you, it's good to be open to experimenting and allowing experience to be a teacher.

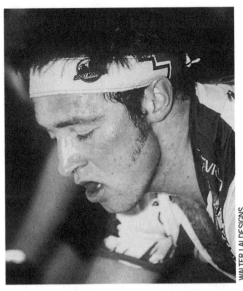

SLOW DOWN YOUR EXHALE TO RELAX YOUR MUSCLES AND LOWER YOUR HEART RATE.

WALTER LAI DESIGNS

SPOT CHECK: EXERCISE-INDUCED ASTHMA

An estimated 15 percent of the athletic population has asthma or exercise-induced bronchospasms (EIB). If you are having difficulty with your breathing during a warm-up, on a challenging ride, or in a race, please check it out with a doctor who understands that even a 10-percent reduction in airways will affect your cycling performance.

There are products that help prevent the symptoms as well as the commonly prescribed Ventolin inhaler that treats the symptoms. Even if you have never had asthma before, intense training exposes you to more environmental irritants and you can develop allergies and asthma after several years.

I recall working with several riders on a cycling team in

Belgium where farmers routinely and repeatedly sprayed the fields with manure. One of the riders developed a disturbing bronchial problem, which improved dramatically as soon as he left that area.

Breath is life. For those of you who are affected with asthma, explore the etiology of your problem; avoid potential environmental irritants, adjust training patterns, be conscious to breathe more through your nose than your mouth, and consult with a knowledgeable sport physician. Remember if you do have trouble breathing, getting uptight will exacerbate the problem. Allow yourself to relax and do what you can to breathe smoothly. Become a breathing expert. Breathing control is vital to your ability to perform successfully.

Turning the wheel—
breathing
for ease, power
...and *less pain*

> "Basic physical strength is necessary. The body's legs and muscles
> have to be there. But you stay on bikes for hours and hours so
> you need to have a little imagination. You need to be intelligent
> and calm. You need to be in control. You need mental control. "
> —Felice Gimondi, Italian pro racer and world champion

> "Breathing is like turning the wheel...as the wheel turns, it
> generates power."
>
> —Dr. Miller

The goal of chapter two is to show you how to use breathing to generate more power, more ease and more control. It's also about learning how to use breathing to deal with difficulty and to reduce pain.

In the last chapter we took a look at how to create a greater sense of calm and control. Many people have difficulty controlling emotions and experiencing ease. Competitive cyclists are no exception, for them the maximum pressure comes just before a race, and in the early stages of a race. At these times, cyclists often feel tense, tight and over-aroused.

The relationship between athletic performance and emotional arousal is depicted in the following graph. What it shows in section A is that as emotional arousal increases, performance improves until it peaks in section B. Thereafter (section C), increases in arousal (over-arousal) lead to a reduction in performance.

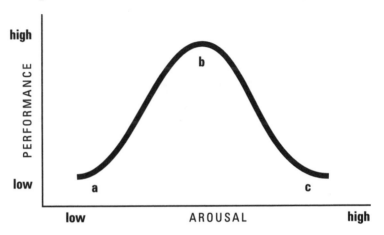

The graph illustrates performance at a given level of emotional arousal or excitement. Many athletes over-arouse under pressure and need to relax or calm down to be at their ideal performance state. There are also those who need to increase their intensity—and sometimes their motivation—in order to perform at their best.

A requirement for consistent, high-level performance is the ability to maintain the ideal level of arousal. The techniques we learned in Chapter One—monitoring tension, releasing and breathing, and pairing positive thoughts with breathing—can help you to create an optimum level of arousal.

In Chapter Two we are going to continue to work with feelings and explore a way to use breathing to generate feelings of power that you can use in climbing, sprinting and initiating an attack. Let's review briefly the "feeling" process we went through in Chapter One.

EXERCISE NO. 1: BREATHING FEELINGS

Sit back and bring attention to your breathing.
Simply notice the rhythm of the breath.
Give yourself time for the breath to flow in.
Give yourself time for the breath to flow out.
As you breathe place a little more emphasis on the in breath.
As you breathe feel yourself drawing in energy.
Allow yourself to imagine energy flowing down through the hips, into the legs and feet.
Feel yourself breathing in energy.
Send energy out through the shoulders into the arms and the hands.
Feel yourself drawing in energy.
Send or imagine energy flowing up the spinal column, into the head and the eyes.
Experience a smooth breathing rhythm.
Draw in energy.
Send energy out to the feet, hands and eyes, like a five-pointed star.

Now imagine riding your bicycle with smoothness and ease. Imagine having good form, being well-positioned on the bike. Imagine breathing in energy and letting it flow through you.

Imagine riding in slow motion with a wonderful sense of ease. Despite the ease with which you ride you are breezing by the other cyclists. Imagine experiencing that good feeling.

Feeling good is fundamental to your enjoyment and success as a racer.

Okay, now experience the breath as a power wheel, spinning.

On the in breath the wheel spins up (a).
On the out breath the wheel spins down (b).
Again, on the in breath the wheel spins up,
and on the out breath the wheel spins down.
Right now you are relaxed, so the wheel turns slowly. As you ride a bicycle, your heart and respiratory rate increase, and the wheel starts to spin faster and faster.
Still, on the in breath the wheel spins up, and on the out breath it spins down.

EXERCISE NO. 2: BREATH SPINS THE WHEEL

Spend a minute or two experiencing your breath as a wheel that is turning.

Then it is important to understand and feel that as the wheel spins it generates power. It's a physiological reality that as you breathe and turn the wheel, you, too, are generating power.

As your heart beats,

and your lungs expand and contract, you are pumping blood, oxygen and energy out through the body.

EXERCISE NO. 3: GENERATING POWER

For a moment experience yourself spinning the wheel.
Breathe in energy, and the wheel
turns up; breathe out, and the
wheel turns down.

Feel the wheel spin up, and draw
in energy and power.
Feel the wheel spin down,
and send out the power.

Last chapter we said that there were three things to focus on with breathing. The first is rhythm; the second is focusing on the in breath; the third is directing energy out into the feet, hands and eyes. The same thing applies to spinning the wheel.

Spinning the wheel is the force that drives your energy.

Allow yourself to feel it.

Imagine breathing in energy
spinning the wheel
and sending out power, like you are a five-pointed star.

Now imagine you are on the road,
and you are riding with a group of people.
It's a competitive situation.
As you ride, experience the feeling of smooth breathing;
experience the feeling of spinning the wheel.

EXERCISE NO. 4: SENDING THE POWER OUT

Feel yourself drawing in power, and then sending it out.

Imagine power flowing throughout the upper body.

Allow energy to flow down through the arms and into the hands.

Experience a firm grip, loose elbows and relaxed shoulders.

Imagine that the upper body is quiet and energy is flowing through it. And allow that energy to flow through the hands and into the handlebars of the bike.

Again, slip back into breathing and spinning the wheel.

Breathe energy in, and send energy out through relaxed shoulders and loose arms, into the hands.

Imagine energy flowing right into the handlebars of the bike.

Now, back to breathing and spinning the wheel.

This time send the energy down,

down through the hips, glutes and quads, and into the feet;

into the power pads in the soles of the feet.

"We've worked with many riders who were told not to move the upper body when cycling, to keep it as still as possible. We want to modify this notion, especially when climbing. We think that if cyclists try to keep their upper body as still as possible they tend to get stiff. We're not advising lots of movement, but you need to move some in order to generate rhythm, flow and power."

—Peg and Saul

Imagine being on the bicycle breathing, spinning the wheel.

Feel your hip and leg action

like a big smooth wheel,

like a locomotive wheel

spinning and generating power.

Draw in energy

send it down.

Imagine your hip and leg like a locomotive wheel

smoothly and easily powering the bike.

Breathe in energy
spin the wheel
send energy up into the eyes.

With your eyes open
anticipate,
evaluate,
read the terrain,
read the riders,
read the action of the race,
feel your energy.

Feeling tired?
Then go deeper into the breathing
and spinning of the wheel.
Generate power
like a five-pointed star.

Send energy into the legs:
smooth, flowing and spinning.

Send energy into the arms:
relaxed shoulders, loose elbows and firm hands.

Send energy into the eyes. It's always eyes open, always aware,
looking for the other strong wheels, and ready to
jump...watching, and riding smart.

Now imagine picking up the pace as you ride.
Begin to spin with a little more speed.
Imagine the feeling of quick feet—
almost dancing on the pedals.

Imagine beginning to climb,
and go deeper into the breathing.

Spin the wheel and send more power down through the drive
train.
Send power through the glutes and quads into the feet.
Imagine generating more power.
Feel that power driving the cranks.

Imagine picking up speed as you head up the incline,
drawing in energy with the in breath
and sending it down through the rest of your body.
And as you send power down,
the spin of the wheel is smooth and strong.

Now imagine that you are moving toward a flatter section,
picking up more speed and using bigger gears with more ease.

Imagine spinning the wheel
and sending power through the hips and quads.
Allow yourself to imagine a continuous flow of energy
as you breath in,
and then exhale from the lower body, from tiger feet—
spinning the wheel with speed and ease...smoothly.

Great.
Always return to spinning the wheel:
feel yourself breathing in energy,
and feel yourself spinning the wheel.

As you ride, create a smooth breathing rhythm.
Focus on drawing in energy and feel the wheel spin up.
Feel yourself generating energy and driving the crank.
Draw in energy and then send it out.

You are spinning the wheel,
generating power,
expanding and contracting your lungs,
pumping the heart,
sending blood, oxygen and energy flowing through your body.

You have a quiet upper body.
But flowing down the legs
and through the drive shaft is the smooth
pumping of your legs and the power that spins the wheels.

You draw in energy and allow it to flow
up the spinal column into your eyes.
Your eyes are wide open;
you are riding smart,
anticipating the course, reading the terrain
and shifting gears.
It's eyes open, reading the other riders, anticipating their moves.
It's eyes open, being aware of what's happening around you.

Imagine approaching an incline.
The flat road you are on is quickly becoming a hill.
You feel yourself mentally and physically preparing for the
climb.
To do that you must go deeper into your breathing.
Spin the wheel.
Generate power
and send it to the crank through the hips, glutes and quads.
Imagine turning that wheel smoothly,
and feel the hill becoming a plain.

Imagine riding on the track.
The track is really smooth and fast.
Imagine that you are doing speed work.
You are breathing, spinning the wheel,
sending the energy down your legs, down like pistons, down,
increasing your revolutions per minute.
You are faster, lighter and more stream-lined.
You are spinning the wheel faster,
generating more speed, more rpms.
Imagine going faster than ever before.

Eric was a successful international racer and a pragmatist. When I consulted with him, he confided that he was a bit leery of sport psychologists. He told me that one of the problems he'd had with a previous "sport shrink" was actually applying the advice he had received—too much of which was complicated and difficult to put to use while riding under pressure. I understood what he meant. If something is to be

USE BREATHING TO CREATE SMOOTHNESS AND ENERGY WHEN RIDING ON THE TRACK.

useful, it had best be presented in a simple way. I asked Eric if the idea of experiencing his breathing as a wheel, spinning that wheel in order to generate power and then sending that power out was simple and useful. "That's great," he replied. "That'll work."

A couple of months later Eric and I again found ourselves talking about sport psychology. Eric said, "You know, I've got to tell you something. That breathing stuff really does work. I was using it in my weight training, and I found that it really increased my power and endurance lifting. It's just a matter of using the generator while riding."

A winning strategy for cycling and life is:

Whatever comes up, use it. In cycling, use it as a cue to stimulate you to spin the wheel.

Everything we experience is a stimulus. Most of the time, the way in which a person reacts to these stimuli is his or her own decision. They are the boss.

Fatigue, incline and acceleration are all stimuli. Fatigue signals that you must go deeper into the breathing, and use breathing to your advantage. An incline signals that you must go a little deeper; spin the wheel smoothly, yet forcefully. When you want to pick up speed, go deeper into breathing; spin the wheel harder and faster, and generate the power necessary to do the hammering.

At the 1983 Pan American Games in Venezuela, I introduced cyclists to some breathing work. Two days later, one of the group members, Damian, was riding a 100 kilometer road race over mountainous terrain in very hot weather. He had not properly hydrated, and after about 50km he began to feel woozy and exhausted. His first reaction was to panic, but that made things worse. After nearly bonking he remembered some of what I had said to him about breathing.

He began to focus on his breathing and began to think about spinning the wheel. "You know," Damian said after the race, "that breathing stuff really works."

"What makes you say that?" I asked.

"Well," he replied, "after I tuned into my breathing, I went another 10 kilometers before I passed out."

PEG You may need to avoid fatigue and stress reactions when things go wrong in a race. Remember, you choose your response to a situation.

Have you ever missed a feed during a race? I have felt the panic of not seeing the support person as we entered the feed zone. Was I going to miss my feed? Now it seems funny to get worked up about that when there are so many options. But at that time, when my coping skills weren't good, I felt that I didn't have any options.

I watched Alison Sydor miss her feed in the final lap at the national championships. She handled it very professionally. She gestured with her hand "Where is my bottle?" but never slowed or spoke. She was a bit bonky at the finish and may have done a faster time, but she never mentioned it to the media and was happy with her win.

There are so many examples of athletes missing feeds but continuing, getting another feed, getting fluid or food from another racer. Connie Carpenter missed a feed in the 1984 Olympic road race where she won the first-ever women's cycling gold medal. Winners don't let a difficult situation affect them. They use it to their advantage. One way you can use a missed feed is as a reminder to go deeper into your breathing and spin the wheel, generate power and focus on the ride ahead of you.

Be aware that as you cycle in any situation—on the road, mountain biking, or on the track—whether you are feeling strong or tired, always use your situation or feeling as a stimulus or cue to remind you to spin the wheel. Increase the flow. There is energy flowing, and you are a five-pointed star.

BLOWING OFF TENSION

Another way to use your breathing that will both increase intensity and reduce tension is something I borrowed from the martial arts. It involves doing some circular breathing—spinning the wheel—and then focussing the energy generated into a series of short punches, which are not directed at anyone. It's as though you are punching through a block of soft, corky wood. Each punch is accompanied by a deep-seated yell. There is a specific way to punch and yell that can be communicated with a little coaching. However, any series of four to eight short, crisp punches accompanied by a deep, chest-centered yell—not throat-centered—can be energizing and at the same time blow off tension. The classic karate yell sound of keii can be used, or you can use whatever sound feels right to you.

A kilo racer's challenge is very high pressure. They have only one chance at each competition, whether it's the world championships, Olympics or nationals. There are no practice heats, no repechage, no two-out-of-three's. There's just one chance. And with the race taking only about one minute to complete, there's intense pressure to make every 10th of a second count. An optimal kilo ride means that you get off the starting line fast, accelerate quickly, and maintain speed for the entire three laps.

As with all races, tension builds as the start time approaches, but because it's a one-timer and a short-duration event, the kilo is especially intense.

Curt was one of the finest kilo racers in the world. We first met at the Pan American Games in Venezuela, and he was on the way up. "I've been training for months," he said, "and it all comes down to 65 seconds. I've got to make sure I'll be there." As part of his mental preparation we worked with a variety of techniques, including breathing, power thoughts and imagery. Curt won a gold medal.

A year later, at the 1984 Los Angeles Olympics, the 19-

year-old Curt was the youngest competitor in the race. Yet he knew exactly what to do to prepare for the event. A couple of hours before the race, Curt used his breathing to relax and recharge (the five-pointed star) and to do some mental rehearsal. In the seconds just before the race, as the pressure built, Curt straddled his bike, tuned into his breathing, focused, and did a modified punch-and-yell routine to energize and blow off excess tension. Then, he drew in a little more power and took off. Curt rode a great race at the

CURT HARNETT USED MANY SPORT PSYCHOLOGY TECHNIQUES INCLUDING BREATHING, POWER WORDS AND AFFIRMATIONS (CH. 3), IMAGERY (CH. 4, 5), SCRIPTING (CH. 4-7) AND MENTAL TOUGHNESS (CH. 8) TO BREAK RECORDS AND WIN MEDALS.

Olympics, a personal best, and won a silver medal. Using his breathing, his determination and his "thunder thighs," Curt went on to win many more medals at the Pan American Games, the Olympics and the world championships.

This technique of circular breathing—punching and yelling—can be effective and fun. Try it. It can be an assertive, expressive way to use your breathing for a performance lift.

One thing you need to add to your ride is a power word. A power word can help you shape energy. The word you choose depends on who you are and what you want. If the feeling you want to experience is smoothness, integration and harmony, use the word smooth or flow.

If the feeling you want is power—if you want to generate energy to initiate an attack or if it's a sprint or a climb—spin the wheel and bring to mind the word strong or power.

If the feeling you want is speed or pace, for a sprint or for the track, spin the wheel and think a word like fast, hammer, pistons or spin.

Power words can and should be added to the feeling component. As one world-class racer said, "The way I say it to myself—'I'm the boss; I make it happen; I'm going for it,' instead of 'Don't get dropped, hang in there'—has a profound effect on my result."

We'll talk more about power thoughts and words in the next chapter.

PAIN

Again and again when we talk to rider, pain comes up as a significant, limiting obstacle to optimal cycling. While every rider experiences some pain, we all have different pain thresholds. And some riders are much more sensitive to pain; they feel it and are bothered by it tremendously.

"I know the pain of cycling can be terrible: in your legs, your chest, everywhere. You go into oxygen debt and fall apart. Not many people outside cycling understand that."
—Greg LeMond,
Three-time Tour de France winner

With training, you can reduce pain's power and be

better prepared to stave it off longer, but pain is always there, and it can bring the best of riders to a halt.

Based on my experience of operating an interdisciplinary pain clinic for several years and consulting with athletes, specifically cyclists, for almost two decades, I've come up with some insights that are useful for dealing with pain.

Pain management

The three basic principles of mind management outlined in chapter one are helpful to review here:

1. The mind is like a television. If you don't like what you think or feel, change the channel. You are the boss.

2. You get more of what you think about. If you think about pain, or how much you hurt, or how painful it's going to be, you intensify the pain.

3. Feelings affect thinking, and thinking affects feeling. Pain is a feeling.

> "Do not give up when you find you have to suffer greatly to get results. Never forget that winners are the ones who can suffer the best. It's the no-hopers who cannot suffer. The inability to suffer is almost always the real reason riders do not succeed in our sport. The person who can suffer the best has the best chance of getting to the top."
>
> —Charles Ruys,
> Australian coach and manager[3]

In chapter four we'll describe pain as one of the three major limiting programs experienced by elite cyclists. Pain causes tension, and tension causes pain.

Pain as a feeling can lead to limited and defensive thinking. Defensive thinking leads to more tension, contraction and pain, which poses the question, what do you do with pain?

The answer is: Use it.

[3] *The Quotable Cyclist*, edited by Bill Strickland, Breakaway Books, New York, NY, 1997.

The first and best pain-management skill is to create more ease. Shift the focus from feelings of pain to your breathing rhythm, power thoughts and performance images. Use pain as a stimulus and a reminder to refocus and go deeper into your breathing.

There are two focusing strategies for dealing with pain: you can either go deeper into it, or turn away from it. In both cases breathing is central to the pain management process.

Going into the pain

When you experience pain, you can use it to go deeper into your breathing. Specifically, think of your breathing rhythm. Pain disorganizes that rhythm. It can cause contraction in the lungs and can shorten your breath, even stopping it momentarily. What's essential is that you regain order with your rhythm, and the easiest and most powerful way to do that is with breathing. As your breathing rhythm begins to strengthen, try to create ease where the pain is located, rather than dis-ease. Imagine sending a soothing energy, or more blood and oxygen into the area. Increase the positive energy flow. If your quads are burning or cramping, think of releasing tension in those muscles and send a soothing energy through that area. You can give a color to that energy depending on what you need: red and gold for warmth, or blue and green for coolness. Release the tension, breathe and send energy through your pain. If you fight it, you will increase tension and magnify the pain. Remember, whatever we resist persists. Use the pain for more rhythm or ease.

Build up your pain tolerance. It's a measure of mental

toughness. Learn and know that you can handle pain better than anybody else. One athlete I worked with as both a rider and a coach, who believed he handled pain better than the competition, used to say, "If it's hurting me, it's killing them."

Reducing pain

It's also possible to send your mind away from the pain. Again, you will need to breathe first and rediscover the rhythm you had before the pain set in; then send your thoughts away from the body or body part that hurts. Direct your mind to the road in front of you, to some landmark such as a bridge, or up to and over the top of the hill. If you see people down the road, think of reeling them in. Think of rhythm. Think of lightness. Focus on a power word such as "strength" or "energy." Contemplate an accomplishment at work. Recall a wonderful holiday you had last year. Use pain as a reminder to breathe and spin the wheel, then refocus on something positive.

Experiment with both these approaches:

• When you experience pain, use it to breathe and spin the wheel, breathe deeper, and move into your pain, calm it, open up the tension and flow with it.

• When you feel pain, use it to breathe and spin the wheel. Focus your thoughts on a landmark, other riders, feeling light, a power word or a pleasant memory.

Caution

Many riders believe that pain is always a good thing, and that hurt is inevitable—a sign that you are doing something "right." But the foundation of optimal cycling is not based on self-destruction. You must nurture your experience and judgment in order to gauge when pain is positively telling you that you are pushing yourself enough, or when it is a signal to be heeded with caution.

HOMEWORK

In chapter two we continued to work with creating feelings of ease and power and related these feelings to riding a bicycle. The homework for this chapter consists of three assignments:

1. Experience at least one 10-minute breathing session every day. Spend a couple of minutes breathing easily and imagining yourself riding your bicycle with ease, speed and excellent form.

2. While riding your bicycle, think about your breath as a "wheel." Especially work at spinning the wheel and generating power when you experience fatigue, climb, initiate a sprint, and do interval training.

3. Define three power thoughts or words that you can use when you ride. Rehearse them several times, and combine them with your breathing exercises prior to reading the next chapter.

HOMEWORK REVIEW

How did your homework go?

Here is feedback from the group of eight riders that attended our eight-week session:

ATHLETE It was good. The breathing definitely helps me to be smooth and calm, and the power words make me think about upcoming efforts I need to make. It's about strategy and thinking ahead. It's a good balance to pair these two.

DR. MILLER Good. I'm glad you experienced that. We develop that idea further in chapter three.

ATHLETE Can you use breathing to recharge if you're tired and you planned to train, or even if you have a race?

PEG When I was a rider I met with Dr. Bruce Ogilvie. We met on Friday afternoons in an office at a local fitness club in Los Gatos, California. I was usually very tired and would have normally napped during that time. Instead, we worked on recharging, which involved me getting into my breathing and then sending energy out though my body. Instead of directing energy out to a five-pointed star, I thought of sending energy out to my chakras (energy centers). I have very vivid recollections of feeling the energy surge through my veins. I heard bolts of electricity shoot through my body, like lightning crackling across the sky. I was definitely reenergized.

So, the answer is "yes." You can use breathing to recharge when you are tired. Practice tuning into your breathing rhythm, inspiring yourself and directing your energy out.

ATHLETE Exactly what are these chakras you are talking about?

DR. MILLER The chakras are energy centers that are believed to exist along the spinal column. There are seven centers. These chakras are located at the base of the spine; the sex organs; the mid-torso; the mid-chest; the throat; in middle of the forehead (which is also known as the third eye); and at the top of the head, or the crown chakra.

There are a number of yoga and meditation techniques

that combine simple breathing with directing attention to these energy centers. One practice is to focus on a chakra, then breathe and tune into the energy at that center. Another technique is to tap the energy at the lower chakras, increase it, and then draw it up to the next higher center. Drawing energy up the spinal column, focusing on each chakra, is supposed to stimulate health, vitality and spiritual awareness. A great deal has been written on the chakras. If you are interested I can recommend a couple of books.[4]

ATHLETE The breathing helped. Something I found energizing was the thought of breathing in pure, fresh energy and breathing out lactic acid. What do you think?

DR. MILLER Sounds good to me. Use your intuition to improve your experience. The ultimate test is how it feels and whether it works for you.

ATHLETE Well, I struggled with actually using the breathing on the bike. What if the breathing as a wheel concept just doesn't work for me?

PEG It often takes time to learn a skill. This is a good one, so I encourage you to keep working on it. You could use imagery to help your breathing. In the last chapter we mentioned being like a steam engine with white steam driving the pistons and the wheels on the locomotive. You might try relating that image to your riding, or the continuity of the

[4] *Energy, Ecstasy and Your Seven Vital Chakras*, Bernard Gunther, Newcastle Publishing, N. Hollywood, CA, 1983.

The Chakras and The Human Energy Field, S. Kargulla M.D. and D.Van Gelden Kurtz, Quest Books, 1997.

Chakra Workout, Barka and Jones, Llewellan Publications, St. Paul, MN, 1996.

The Chakras, CW Leadbeater, Quest Books-Theosophical Publications (original 1927), 1997.

waves, the image of the waves continuously pounding on the shore and wearing away any obstacles. Images can be very helpful. We'll work with images in depth in chapter four.

SPOT CHECK: REPLENISHING

Replenishing yourself under pressure is as much an art as a science. Something that can't be overlooked is the physical need to eat and hydrate. When we burn our limited glycogen stores and cool off by perspiring, our mental capabilities are diminished if the levels are not replenished. It takes as little as 2 percent of body weight in water loss for this to happen, and 6-percent of water loss is a dangerous level for bodily function. So, make sure you hydrate and rehydrate.

Consider it a tactic then, to rehydrate and replenish glycogen during rides and races. A rule of thumb is to go through one water bottle per hour. Test how much you need and in what forms—energy bars, gels, dried fruit, electrolyte drinks— during training and less important races. High temperatures, altitude and humidity can alter those amounts. Remember this is essential for long rides. The best time to fully replenish is during the first two hours after riding and racing.

Carbohydrates

People who do not eat complex carbohydrates may find themselves unable to sustain the energy levels required by cycling.

PEG During one summer Olympic Games, I coached an athlete to her peak by advising her to eliminate sweets and, instead, eat complex carbohydrates the week before the event. She was also dehydrated but followed the example of her teammates, sipping water often. Before that she could not handle the training load that the others could.

Cyclists who do not eat enough protein can also experience a drop in energy. Loading up on carbohydrates, they may feel sleepy and find that their long-term recovery is poor. If you have questions about your diet, consult with a sports medicine specialist, nutritionist or health-care expert who is knowledgeable about competitive sport. But don't overlook the importance of becoming an expert on what replenishment and diet works best for you.

Record this information in your training journal. Support your hard training by looking after your body.

Iron men and women

During a seminar I was conducting at a cycling training camp, Barrie Shepley, Canada's national triathlon team coach, shared a valuable tip with the group regarding focus for long races such as the Ironman. In many races that require an athlete to perform at his or her peak for more than nine hours, athletes tend to lose focus, space out and forget to attend to their physical needs such as fluid replenishment. They also forget to make important mental adjustments.

Barrie suggested that his athletes set their watch to beep every 10 to 15 minutes. With each beep they are trained to "perform a scan"—an internal and external bodily read. While cycling, the check list may include: replenishment needs for fluid and food, posture on the bike, pace (pick it up or slow it down), what internal programs are running (self talk or images), and externals such as location, position in the field, who is doing what, and the weather. Without training athletes to scan the situation and make adjustments, many would fail to do those basic things that support their performance.

Power
thoughts

"Your thoughts shape your reality. Think power thoughts like 'smooth and fast,' 'I can,' and 'I corner well.' You get more of what you think about."

—Dr. Miller

"When every racer is physically at their best, the difference between them is how they think and what they say to themselves."

—Peg

The goal of chapter three is to become more aware of how thought can influence performance, and to develop a program of power thoughts that will really enhance your cycling experience.

In the first two chapters we emphasized the importance of creating "right feelings," specifically, feelings of ease and power, and how to use breathing to help you to do that. It was also suggested that you control your feelings in order to manage your mind.

In the next two chapters, we want to talk more about focus and programming. Focus is what you consciously tune into on your mental television. It's about the thoughts, feelings and images you bring to mind that help you perform.

Everyone is a performer. As a cyclist, you will perform better by improving focus and programming.

POWER WORDS

At the end of chapter two we introduced the idea of "power words." We talked about how the words "smooth" and "flow" can help create a good feeling as you ride.

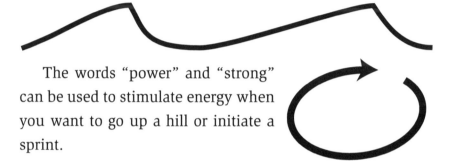

The words "power" and "strong" can be used to stimulate energy when you want to go up a hill or initiate a sprint.

The words "spin" and "fast" can help when you want more speed.

Power words can also be used to build or strengthen self-esteem. When we spoke about managing your mental television, we said "you're the boss." You control the situation. You control your thoughts and feelings in any situation.

When you think about breathing and controlling the mind it can be useful to have a power word or phrase like "I'm the boss." Thinking "I'm the boss" or just the word "boss" can remind you that you are in control and reinforce the sense that whatever comes up, you can handle it.

Similarly, saying "I'm okay" means "I can handle it."

One thing that differentiates high and low self-esteem people is that high self-esteem people enjoy a challenge. They like to compete. The words "boss" and "okay" can remind you of your response-ability and help you anticipate and respond well to a challenge.

Two other power words are "aware" and "eyes." Both are reminders to keep eyes open and be alert as you ride—to anticipate the terrain: to know the hills, the flats, the corners, rough spots and obstacles.

Eyes can also help you to anticipate the other riders: to know who is charged and ready to go, and who is tired.

A RIDER USING HIS "EYES" TO SEE THE SITUATION FROM THE FRONT OF THE PACK.

The word "crafty" is another word some riders have used to remind them to focus on their situation and to use everything. Crafty means that your eyes are open and you know who's where, and what's happening. Crafty also means push and pace—use energy wisely and efficiently.

If you have seen people down the road ahead of you, the thought "reel them in" is a power phrase and image that can give some direction to your energy.

"Reeling them in" is about intention. Intention is a powerful mental force that you can put to work for you. The word intention comes from a root word that means "sending out the mind." "Reel them in" can express the feeling and image of sending out your mind, your intention, and hooking the other riders, drawing them in and closing the gap.

PEG Some riders really exaggerate this concept, using a fishing rod image to reel in their minute man in a time trial or a break that's up the road. They visually "hook" their sights on the other rider and use their cranks as the fishing reel, spinning faster to "reel them in."

Other riders think about who is chasing them and are motivated by the fear of being overtaken. We believe it is always better to project forward. Keep your focus ahead to a point at which you can project your power and ride aggressively, rather than looking over your shoulder and riding out of fear, which produces tension.

Many famous races have been lost by a competitor who looks for their opponent, only to get nipped at the line. I was taught to never look across the track at my challenger in the pursuit event. Looking takes your focus off your task at hand

and allows the mind to wander to thoughts about who will win. Keep focused on your race until you are over the finish line.

Power words should be so strong that they create a feeling and a picture that increases your power, direction and potential.

There are many kinds of power words you can use. There are tactical power words. If you are going very fast downhill the word "tuck" can create an aerodynamic position that gives you less resistance and more speed. It's important that you select a few power words that work for you.

There are two power words that I have used in every sport, and they certainly apply in cycling: "attack" and "smooth." Attack and smooth are the yin and yang of riding and racing. Either you are putting the pedal to the metal and pushing to go as fast as you can—in "attack"—or you are smoothing it out, giving yourself more flow, which is pacing and balancing and will ultimately lead to more efficiency and speed—"smooth."

attack   smooth

In events such as downhill mountain bike racing, "attack" and "smooth" are extremely useful because the whole race is about attacking and then instantly switching gears to "smooth," finessing, controlling and handling the bike well through difficult rough spots, rocks and down sharp drops in the course. The result is smooth, handle it, smooth, flow, feeling the bicycle—over and around the obstacles. Then, as

TINKER JUAREZ USES "SMOOTHING"
TO GO FASTER ON DOWNHILLS.

the course flattens out again it becomes attack, attack, attack, turn the wheel, accelerate, hammer, push, go....

Success is directly related to your ability to anticipate the shift from attacking to going smoothly, and to react well at the right time.

It's the same on the road. There are times when you are pacing, smoothing and working on good flow and an efficient use of energy. Then, as you move into an incline or into a sprint situation, you think "attack" and become aggressive.

With training, the power word "attack" can create a feeling that will spark you to spin the breathing wheel deeper and push for power. "Smooth" can remind you to smooth out that flow of energy through the body. And smooth can also mean speed.

PEG How do you know when to smooth and when to attack?

There are two types of cues for "attack." One type is dictated by the terrain of the course. Difficult terrain such as climbs, open windy roads, technical trails and tight turns requires more physical effort and skill.

The successful rider pours effort into these challenges and avoids wasting energy in futile efforts such as attacking on straight descents where others can easily follow or little time can be gained.

The second cue for "attack" is any moment of strategic action in a race such as the final lap, prime laps, or counter-attacking some- one else's aggressive move. The

> *"I've worked on my downhilling, and I've gotten a lot smoother. Go smoother and you go fast."*
> —Tinker Juarez, Olympian and U.S. mountain-bike national champion

successful rider conserves energy by "smoothing" between efforts and puts more energy into well-timed attacks. For example,

instead of:	do this:
riding out in the wind	use other's wheels to move up
putting out numerous attacks	wait and put more into one attack
attacking on the downhill	attack out of a corner or at the top of a climb
pulling at the front	attack from the top third of the group

And the list goes on…. The more you practice reading the terrain and the action of the race, the better you can get at predicting the final outcome. The goal is to recognize win- ning moves and take the opportunities to make these moves.

By using visualization, you can experience races in your head and practice your response to the attack and smooth cues. The faster your actual response time, the bigger advan- tage you have over your opponents. Athletes who "think too much" or listen to negative inner dialogue ("I'm tired," "I'm not sure I can do this now") often miss the moment.

TO SUMMARIZE:

1. Use positive affirmations and breathing to counter any negative inner dialogue.

2. Use cue words like "eyes open" and "attack" to take the focus off you and get back into the race.

3. Plan many options for how to respond to the action of the race.

4. Make the race more of a game. Be a hunter. Be in the moment. Be a cat ready to pounce.

The use of power words can be extremely helpful in dealing with the pressure and pain that is a part of racing. Let me give you an example about how I used power words to help a group of cyclists prepare for the Olympics, which resulted in them riding an incredible race.

In preparation for the 1988 Olympics, I worked with Canada's team time trial riders for a week at the beginning of their season in early March, showing them techniques for greater ease, focus and control. They left to train and race in Texas, Great Britain, Belgium, Germany and the Canadian Rockies. When I met them again in British Columbia in early July they were in excellent shape. They were well coached and well-conditioned, and they were riding with very good equipment. For a sport psychologist that's ideal. You can influence the psyche of an athlete who's not in very good shape, but in a physically demanding 100km race, having motivation and focus without the necessary physical conditioning or proper equipment wouldn't make much difference. However, when athletes are physically and technically prepared, getting them "out of their minds" about what they can't do can make a tremendous difference in their race performance.

Once the Olympic team had been selected by the Canadian Cycling Association, the Olympic Committee—an independent body—had to approve the selection. Its job was to ensure that the people sent to the Olympic Games would be competitive, and they refused to send performers—even if they were the best in the country—if they were not up to world standards. In the TTT, the Canadian best record time was 2:06:40. The Olympic Committee set a standard of 2:05:30. In effect, they said to these prospective Olympians either they had to take 1:10 off their best-ever time or they weren't going to the Olympics. That was the challenge.

As usual, I began showing them how to release and breathe, just as I described it in chapters one and two. We worked individually and in groups. As the riders became more relaxed and focused, I asked them what thoughts, images and feelings—their inner voice "programs"—they experienced that limited them when they raced.

Essentially they described three "limiting thoughts or programs." They had to do with fear, pain and difficulty. At the time, I thought their response was specific to cyclists, but in time I realized it applies to us all.

Fear

The fear the racers spoke about was a fear of losing control, of breaking down, of failure, of embarrassment, and of crashing and getting injured. For most of us, fear is a high-frequency performance thought. It's one that can mobilize us for action, or as we said in chapter two, it can cause contraction, limit breathing and cut down power.

Pain

Pain was a second limiting program. In chapter two we explained that the pain experienced in cycling is a physical pain so intense at times that a rider can't continue to race. Some even pass out on their bicycles. Then there is the psychic pain that both racers and non-riders experience in relation to the possibility of a failed performance. Psychic pain threatens the ego. Like physical pain, it also causes contraction, limits breathing and cuts down power.

Difficulty

Difficulty is the third limiting thought or program. "It's hard." Under race circumstances, thoughts and feelings like "this is hard," "it's impossible," "there's no way," and "I can't do it," also cause contraction, limit breathing, increase drag and cut down power. I asked each rider to define a single thought that they could tune into whenever they experienced fear, pain or difficulty on their mental TV. The thought was to be a simple and powerful one—a single word that was personally meaningful and that stimulated a feeling and gave them power. It had to be simple and brief. The stress and fatigue of a race can express itself like static or snow on a TV set, making it difficult to focus. We wanted a power word that would be comprehensible and useful under pressure.

Each racer selected a different word. Brian,[5] the team's leading racer chose the word "more." Whenever he experienced pain, fatigue, self-doubt or negativity, he would think "more," turn the wheel and push a little harder, a little longer

[5] The TTT team consisted of Olympic silver medalist, Pan American Games double gold medalist, and Team Saturn captain Brian Walton, plus Yvon Wadell, Chris Koberstein, and David Spears.

DAVID SPEARS, LEFT, AND SAUL MILLER, DISCUSS HIS COPING STRATEGY PRIOR TO
THE TEAM TIME TRIAL SQUAD SHATTERING THE NATIONAL RECORD AND QUALIFYING
FOR THE OLYMPICS.

or a little faster. Yvon chose the power word "smooth." He
was a big man who knew that under pressure he would often
tighten up and end up having to work harder to accomplish
the same result. Chris chose the power word "machine." He
wanted to see himself as inhuman and impervious to pain,
doubt and difficulty. Whenever he noticed himself tuning
into a limiting thought or feeling, Chris would take a breath,
draw in energy, turn the wheel, think "machine" and accelerate. Dave chose the word "fast." It sparked in him the
image to be lighter, tougher, more aggressive and stream-
lined. He brought that power word to mind whenever he felt
stressed.

Part of their psychological training addressed dealing effectively with the considerable pain, tension and difficulty pro-
duced by that grueling event. I explained to each rider that the

65

natural reaction to pain, tension and difficulty is to contract, to tighten up and to try to hold on. I repeatedly explained to each racer that it is much easier to be aggressive than it is to hold on. Holding on doesn't change anything. It just means that you attempt to ride the race in the state of being tense and contracted. And it is much more difficult to be fast and to endure in that contracted, limited state. Along with the thought of being aggressive, we spent a lot of time working with breathing and release—changing channels—so that when a racer felt pain they would use it to focus on their breathing, on turning the wheel, and on their positive power word.

In the race the team went out very fast. After 20km Chris said he started to feel pain and began to think, "I hurt." Then he thought, "just hold on." When he realized what he was thinking, he reminded himself "It's easier to be aggressive than to hold on," and he went deeper into his breathing, refocused on the word "machine" and picked up his pace. Again, about 70km into the race Chris became focused on and locked into pain. Again, the negative thoughts followed: "I can't continue," and "just hold on." Again, he realized what he was doing. Refocused on his breathing and on being like a "machine," he rode right through the pain. He rode a great race. The whole team did.

What makes this story particularly interesting is the bottom line. The riders went out at a fast pace and stayed focused and aggressive throughout the race. Dave, Chris and Yvon all mentioned to me afterward that they were hurting and thought, "I can't do it. I can't go on." When they noticed themselves tuning into that feeling or thought, they remembered to go deeper into their breathing, to turn the wheel, to change channels, to generate more power and then refocus on their power word. The end result was they rode the 100km distance in 1:51:10. Their time was 15 minutes and 30 seconds faster than the previous Canadian record—an unofficial world record in that event.

THE RECORD-BREAKING CANADIAN TTT TEAM IN ACTION.

What's remarkable is that it wasn't a new team of superstars imported from another part of the planet or the galaxy. Three of the four racers had been part of the team that set the 2:06:40 mark the year before. What was different now was that all the key elements were in place. They were well coached, which is to say, the right people had been selected, they knew what to do and they were in excellent shape. And, they were trained to manage their minds aggressively, to change channels in the face of limiting thoughts and feelings and to stay tuned into winning programs including their power words.

An aside to this power word-excellence story involves one of the alternate team racers from the four-man back-up team. This particular racer didn't perform well when he rode for the national team. When he raced for his club, he was daring and aggressive. But as soon as he put on that national team jersey he became tentative and defensive. Instead of "going for it" his focus became "don't make a mistake." Instead of projecting his mind forward and out along the course and "reeling them in," he focused on his feet, counted his pedal revolutions and made sure he didn't pull less than his share.

The dominant thought patterns he had acquired and ran were "don't let them down," "they're watching," and "they're counting on you." His focus was the ubiquitous "them." Consequently, the program he selected to focus on was "f—- 'em." Whenever he felt himself tighten up and think a negative thought, he'd take a breath, draw in power, think "f—- 'em" and turn the wheel.

An amusing aspect of the story is that I asked each of the riders to write out their "word" and stick it onto the back of the seat of the bicycle in front of them so that as they rode on that wheel, they would have a visual reminder of their program. The Olympic Trials was held on a blocked-off section of the Trans-Canada Highway outside of Vancouver. Prior to the race a crowd of cycling enthusiasts, friends and supporters milled around examining the state-of-the-art bicycles. With curiosity, they read the words on the back of each seat, "more," "smooth," "machine," "fast," and then "f—- 'em." On seeing the last stimulus, the spectators sometimes did a double-take and looked at the rider attached to the bicycle with the obscenity, and said something critical or looked critically at the rider. The rider inevitably flushed, and said, "It's not my word." But, of course, no one had any idea what he was talking about.

EXERCISE NO. 1: PICKING POWER WORDS

Last session we asked you to select, and train, with three words that related to the way you wanted to feel when you ride. Now let's define and add a few more words that will stimulate your feelings and focus, give you a clearer picture of what to do...plus more energy as you ride or race.

You may want to select an aerodynamic word that will give you less resistance on descents. One suggestion is "tuck," but feel free to create your own.

You may think of a word or phrase for those times when you see someone or a group ahead of you down the course and you want to reel them in. You can use "reel" or come up with another word.

Think of a word you can use when you want to be more aware of the situation, the terrain or the other riders. You may think "alert" or "eyes."

In my experience the most helpful power words in bicycle racing are "attack" and "smooth."

Incorporate a few power words into your cycling. Select words that appeal to you and that are clear and strong enough to give you an image or a feeling. For them to have any potency or "juice" in an intense race situation you have to train them into your mind in practice. That means, define and select a few key words before you go out to ride, and consciously and repeatedly use these words at appropriate times as you train until they become part of your cycling self-talk.

Remember, "boss" can be a reminder that you're in control; you can handle it. "Eyes" or "crafty" can be a stimulus for awareness or a mental edge. "Tuck" for downhill can remind you of the form to descend like an arrow. You may just want to use "attack" and "smooth," to push and pace yourself throughout the race.

CANADIAN NATIONAL CHAMPION MARK WALTERS LEADS AN ATTACK.

PEG Another way of thinking about smooth and attack is by applying it when politics and self-serving relationships come into play. At any moment you can decide what is important to fight for ("attack") and what to accept ("smooth") and let go of. There are many examples of athletes who conflict with coaches, selection procedures or officials' decisions.

One way to smooth is to put the issue on hold and let time—and possibly more information—provide a different perspective. Another approach to smoothing is to defer, to get "an agent" to handle it for you. Use rider's reps, managers or another rider to take up your cause so that you can focus on cycling. Techniques called "treeing," "parking" or "filing" can also be used. These are expressions for putting the worry up in a tree, parking it off on the side or filing it while you deal with more important things at hand. You can always get it down or call it back later, when it may be a better time to "attack."

It is often athletes who are borderline who get caught up in these problems. They may be vying for the last spot on a team, have had marginal performance and are unsatisfied with selection criteria or choices. These individuals would be better served accepting the situation by "smoothing" and focusing their energy on "attacking" and improving their performance or themselves.

Affirmations and power thoughts

In addition to power words there are "power thoughts" that you can say to yourself that can be beneficial in nurturing a positive mindset for training and competing...and for life in general.

Remember, you get more of what you think about. Affirmations are simply positive statements of what you want to create and what you are in the process of manifesting. They can relate to skill, conditioning, strategy and attitude.

For example: "I deserve to be in that breakaway," "I focus well in time trials," "I am good at technical mountain biking," "I ride smoothly and steadily." By repeating these thoughts to yourself you can grow a more positive mindset that can nurture optimal effort and a greater sense of well being.

I encourage athletes to take a breath and say their power thoughts. I frequently make tapes for athletes combining relaxation and breathing with their power thoughts. The process involved in selecting these thoughts begins with you exploring how you want to feel, defining what you want to achieve and then creating an affirmation or power thought that you feel comfortable and positive about saying to yourself.

CYCLING AFFIRMATIONS

Here are some thoughts to repeat to yourself. Select the ones that feel good to you and give you what you want. After each thought take a breath. Remember, thoughts precede action, and repetition builds strength. The following is a list of affirmations that the Canadian Cycling Team used at a pre-Olympic training camp:

- *I am the boss. I control my programming. I have a personal connection to unlimited energy and power. Anytime, anywhere, with a breath I can feel stronger, calmer and quicker.*
- *I am a power channel. Energy flows through me like a star.*
- *I am electric. I am jet-powered.*
- *I am quick and strong as a cat.*
- *I use my speed and timing perfectly.*
- *I am a big cat—tiger (cheetah or panther).*
- *I am a power machine. I am smoothness and power.*
- *My breath is a power pump.*
- *Some free breathing and a little adrenaline is like jet fuel.*
- *I keep going like the ocean waves. I am consistent and tire-*

less like the ocean waves.
- *I can depend on my legs for speed and power.*
- *I pedal big gears with speed and smoothness.*
- *I am one with my bike.*
- *I am mentally tough.*
- *My mind is a force I use to make things happen.*
- *The status quo isn't good enough. I am committed to riding 100 percent.*
- *I use everything for more power.*
- *I use the great ones. I use the other racers.*
- *I use pain as positive feedback.*
- *I use it all to make me tougher, faster and hungrier to win.*
- *I deserve to express 100 percent of my ability. I use the wind.*
- *I ride the wind.*
- *I cut the wind like a knife.*
- *I find something positive in every situation.*
- *I use the tough days, the hills and the class riders to push me to be tougher, stronger and faster.*
- *I want to be the best I can be.*
- *I take strength from drafting others.*
- *I get strength from challenging and catching others.*
- *I am a winner.*
- *I enjoy winning.*
- *I am excited about doing what nobody else can do.*
- *I have everything I need to be a gold medal racer.*
- *Self-love is allowing myself to win.*
- *I deserve to express 100 percent of my ability.*
- *I forgive myself for limits I may have imposed upon myself in the past.*

- *As I go out to race I remember to review my goals.*
- *I recall the feelings I've had on great days.*
- *I tune out irrelevant thoughts and worries.*
- *I breathe in energy and power. I allow it to flow through my body as if I were a star.*
- *I see myself performing well, and I love it.*
- *Hellen Keller once said, "Life is a great adventure or nothing at all." I am excited about the opportunity to give 100 percent. I am going for it. I deserve it. I'm going to take it.*
- *There is nothing to prevent me from giving 100 percent.*
- *I use everything.*
- *I am aggressive about converting my weakness into strength and power.*
- *I welcome the opportunity that my experience provides to develop myself 100 percent.*
- *I balance aggression and hard work with relaxation, breathing and recharging every day.*
- *I deserve to feel good. Feeling good and recharging is an important part of my total preparation.*
- *As I relax and breathe I am aware of my personal connection to power.*
- *I am aware that I belong and that I don't have to prove anything to anyone.*
- *I am committed to doing whatever is necessary to serve the team and achieve our goal.*
- *We are winners.*
- *I am a winner.*

SPEED AFFIRMATIONS

The following is a list of personal affirmations I used while working with a kilo racer at the world championships. He went on to set a flying 200-meter record. After reading each thought take a breath, and let it sink in. Remember, repetitions build strength.

- *Power is the essence.*
- *I am tapped into an unlimited supply of power.*
- *I am a power machine.*
- *I have power pads, a cat's feet.*
- *My legs are pistons.*
- *With each breath I draw in power.*
- *I send power out in front of me, and down my legs and feet.*
- *I cut through air like a knife.*
- *I am ease and power.*
- *The more I ride the faster I go.*
- *I am light and strong, like a big cat.*
- *I ride faster and faster.*
- *Pain is power.*
- *I use everything.*
- *Nothing distracts me.*
- *My focus is energy in, energy out, ease and power, faster and faster.*
- *I deserve to express all of my ability. I deserve to be as great as I can be.*

EXERCISE No. 2: SELECT AFFIRMATIONS

Review the affirmations in the two preceding examples. Determine which ones may work for you by selecting those that relate to your situation, that address your strengths or aspects of cycling that you want to develop, or those that just feel good.

Select the six to eight affirmations or power thoughts that would most help you to become a more powerful, positive rider.

Write them down and repeat them to yourself often.

You can say your affirmations to yourself or write them in the first person. The first person is personal and powerful.

I am smooth. I am a power machine.

Or you can affirm in the second person. In our day-to-day lives, people usually address us in the second person. It's both effective and pleasant to hear positive things said about us in the second person.

You are a star. You use everything.

I often make tapes for athletes that repeat the affirmations both in the first and second person. Words are like food for the spirit. They can nurture us. Just as you wouldn't eat food that you don't like, it's important that you say things to yourself that feel good and that give you power.

Repetition of these words and phrases builds strength. Repeat these power words and thoughts to yourself frequently. Develop a positive mental focus and attitude. In relaxing and challenging situations, take a breath and affirm the positive.

PEG Remember to use breathing when you are repeating affirmations or imaging with power thoughts. The positive feeling has to come first, or you could be repeating these things and not believing them. If you match the positive feeling with the positive thought, you create a loop that feeds itself with positive energy.

HOMEWORK

There are three assignments:

1. Continue to work with your breathing and feelings. Combine breathing and the five-pointed star image during interval training or on a ride this week.

2. Define six to eight affirmations. Repeat them daily—in the morning, before riding and during riding. Some people tape a list of their favorite affirmations to the mirror and look at themselves while repeating them. Give it a try.

3. Review several past races or rides in terms of smooth and attack. For every part of the course label it "smooth" or "attack." Do the same for your overall strategy of the race, noting where to smooth and where to attack with your energy.

HOMEWORK REVIEW

Here are more of Peg's observations and comments:

1. The breath as a wheel idea seems to help riders prepare for a hard effort. It reminds them to breathe deeply, to focus on the task, to prepare for some intensity, and what's necessary to sustain the effort.

The five-pointed star provides access to a source of power, which can be used to get strength from, or direct strength to. For some, the five-pointed star is a reminder to trust. It's a check that they are physically prepared and that their bodies can do this effort. Perhaps the star could even be six-pointed like the Star of David, because a cyclist connects to a bike with their two feet, two hands, their seat and their mind.

2. Some affirmations stimulate the rider's visual imagination, stretching reality and reflecting what the rider wants to be or experience. For example, "I time trial like Miguel Induráin," or "I fly on descents." Riders seemed to find it motivating to invoke these images. Others used affirmations that related to info they gained from workouts, such as "I can do nine 1km efforts" as a reminder before a final sprint that they can do that one effort since in training they did it nine times.

3. In the exercises we have been doing so far, most riders think of themselves riding solo, and are less aware of the other riders. When the riders worked with "smooth" and "attack," several commented that the attack mode could be instigated by other riders' attacks and their effort could be a part of that surge or going after it in a counter attack. Several riders began to think more about riding with other riders. Until now, most have been more concerned with their own feelings of ease or discomfort on the bike. "Open eyes" is a good cue for them to be aware of the entire ride or race, which opens them to the fun and games. It stimulates them to respond to the outer game instead of listening to inner dialogue so much. As they become aware of who is making moves, who is riding strongly and who's is a good wheel to be on, they grow their awareness of what is happening.

SPOT CHECK: BIKE FIT AND POSITION

Being properly fitted to your bike is essential. Why?

1. It prevents injuries. You do thousands of pedal strokes in each ride. A one-hour ride at 90 revolutions per minute demands 5400 pedal strokes. So, if your seat is too low by just a few millimeters, that error is magnified by the number of repeated pedal strokes. Even one ride in the wrong position can damage knees or aggravate other muscles, ten-

> *"LeMond was a study in perfect riding posture and bike fit. He did not fight the bicycle."*
> *—Edmund Burke*
> *U.S. team consultant and author*

> *"Of all the sports, cycling is the one that requires the most perfect match of man and machine. The more perfect the match the more perfect the result."*
> *—Paul Cornish*
> *U.S. road racer; first cross-country record holder: 13 days, 5 hours, 20 minutes*

dons, ligaments and joints, as well as other body parts.[6]

2. It is difficult to perform the necessary skills when you don't sit properly on your bike. If you can't reach the pedals, you can't pedal properly. If your handlebars are too wide or stem too long you'll have difficulty maneuvering in corners, pacelines or technical terrain. So, if you are having trouble with some skills, check your position.

3. It's difficult to focus on going faster or smoother if staying seated in uncomfortable. Helmets also need checking for comfort and visibility.

4. When all of the above are in place, more energy can be put into being faster and lasting longer on rides or at races. Barry Lycett, a former national coach and expert "bike-fitter," explained the cycling power stroke with reference to a clock.

---

[6] A prominent American urologist recently made the controversial comment that cycling led to genital numbness and advised people not to cycle. When Canada's national cycling team physician, Dr. Gloria Cohen, was asked about the urologist's remarks, she said that pressure on nerves or blood vessels can lead to temporary numbness...and if it is prolonged and repetitive the numbness could become chronic. If it persists, see your physician. Cohen believes it was really a matter of bike fit and that, generally, a seat adjustment is required. Have an experienced coach set or check your position, seat and cleats.

The crank arms are like the hands on the clock. To get maximum power, push from the one o'clock position all the way through to the seven o'clock position. The other pedal does the same. When your seat is too high or too low, you reduce your power time on each revolution.

If you are having trouble with comfort or skills on your bike, it may not just be a mental problem—check to make sure there isn't a bike fit problem. Occasionally, you will face the opposite situation, knowing, for example, that a borrowed bike doesn't fit properly. Use positive affirmations with breathing to get yourself through the ride to the best of your abilities.

PEG Some of my favorite coping skills come from knowing that it is the rider's heart that always makes them come through, and creating affirmations like "I can do this for 50km," "the underdog wins," or "I love riding my bike, no matter what." Imagine creating your own story about overcoming a bike fit problem to win a race.

Power
imagery

*"Imagination is more powerful than the will.
Your images are a blueprint that shape your
performance. See it. Believe it. Do it.
Run positive pictures on your mental TV."*
—Dr. Miller

*"I imagine I am an eagle soaring,
watching, ready to attack."*

—Peg

The goal of chapter four is to explore four different approaches to imagery that will improve cycling performance, and to develop an imagery program that enhances training, performance and well-being.

Let's explore imagery and how high-performance images can help your cycling. Images are the basis of mind. We experience images before we use words. The mind thinks in images. It is an essential aspect of being able to focus. If a picture is worth a thousand words, dynamic imagery can be a training manual.

There are three basic kinds of images: mental rehearsal, imagining the end result, and using animal imagery.

MENTAL REHEARSAL

The first kind of imagery has to do with mentally rehearsing the event. Mental rehearsal means practicing in your mind the things you want to do on the bicycle in competition or on a challenging ride.

EXERCISE NO. 1: MENTAL REHEARSAL

One of the best ways to mentally rehearse something is to imagine yourself riding a bicycle on a course you have ridden before. First, you must relax. Take a couple of breaths. Feel the waves flowing in and out. Relaxing and breathing improves the quality and clarity of your imagery.

Now, see yourself on a challenging ride. Imagine feeling good and handling the bike well. You feel strong and smooth. Relax, breathe and experience those feelings.

Warm up your mental rehearsal by beginning your imagery with the easy parts. Then gradually imagine you are going through some of the more difficult parts of the course or the race. See and feel yourself handling these parts well—feeling smooth and powerful. Imagine yourself riding with good technique, using good strategy and making all the right decisions.

EXERCISE NO. 2: REHEARSING PERFORMANCE

Now let's assume that you want to mentally rehearse for a challenging upcoming race. Imagine, for example, that it is a cross-country mountain bike race (see chapter six for templates of other types of races).

You have seen the course and you have a clear memory

of it. Picture it in your mind. Picture the start. You want to get off to a good start, to generate some speed and jump and, if possible, to get away from the pack.

Imagine building up a charge just before the race is about to start.

Imagine straddling your bike at the starting line, breathing, turning the wheel and generating some power.

As the race starts, imagine yourself turning the wheel with power and speed. You are not forcing it.

It's an attack situation, but you stay relaxed as you draw in power and send it down and out, turning the wheel, picking up speed. You are the tiger. You are sprinting. You have good power. You are driving your legs.

As you get farther away with that first group you begin to scan the terrain, eyes open; you read the terrain and your position. You are in the lead group. You begin to smooth things out. You start to lower your heart rate. You want to pace yourself.

Attack becomes smooth.

You anticipate aspects of the terrain, see them and react smoothly, shifting gears, having a good feel through the rough spots, accelerating and attacking as the course demands or dictates.

Visualize yourself riding the course as you want to, as you anticipate it, through an area of rocky terrain, smoothing it, being one with the bike—like a mountain lion or goat picking your way through the difficult areas with good control, controlling speed with the front brake, and controlling direction with the rear brake. You are handling the bike well—

being at one with the bicycle.

Create a mental picture of the course on which you will be riding. Make notes and sketches if that helps you. Note the rough spots; then imagine you are smoothing it out and handling the bike through these challenging spots with more touch and feel. Note the flats and the areas with speed potential. Imagine moving into these flatter areas anticipating, turning the wheel, "attacking" and generating speed.

Finish visualizing your ride with the most effort on the final lap.

Finish, feeling good about your ride.

Repetition builds strength

Frequent practice with mental rehearsal will help you to develop your skills and increase your awareness of any course, so that you are better able to read, anticipate and react in any situation.

While mental rehearsal is useful in all kinds of bicycle racing, it is probably most important in downhill mountain biking. A downhill mountain-bike racer must have a clear mental picture of the course and mentally rehearse the entire course prior to the race so that they can see it in their minds. In working with downhillers, I usually begin by highlighting the difficult areas first, helping them to see themselves handling these areas, then, seeing themselves getting off to a good start, smoothing down, anticipating the rough spots and handling them with ease. I ask them to identify the feelings they want to have, deciding where they are going to push down and where they are going to go around a rock, anticipating, then seeing the speed spots where they can attack and generate more speed. Linking these pieces together helps the racer see the course the way they want to experience it.

PEG Mental rehearsal is as important to optimal cycling as physical practice. Sometimes people don't actually perform the physical skill correctly. These skill tips that follow are fundamental. To improve your cycling it's important to execute these skills properly and mentally rehearse doing them.

EXERCISE NO. 3: REHEARSING SKILLS

Visualize yourself doing any of the following skills required for your event:

ON THE ROAD

- think about having good form on the bike
- look ahead
- elbows are lowered and loose
- shoulders are relaxed
- there is quickness in your legs
- each muscle is used in succession for an equal amount of time so that the pedal strokes flow one into another
- you increase cadence and gearing to go faster

THROUGH CORNERS

- you are looking ahead to where you want to be when you exit the turn
- you are leading with your eyes focused at the front of the pack so that you carry speed and momentum through the turn effortlessly
- let go of the brakes

WHEN CLIMBING SEATED

- you are sitting up tall in order to open your breathing
- your hands are on the top of the bars
- you are pulling back on the handlebars with every pedal stroke, right and left
- you push down on the pedals and follow through by dropping your heels, using your torso, quads, hamstring and calves

WHEN CLIMBING STANDING

- you prepare for the incline by shifting to a bigger gear
- your hands move to the brake hoods, pulling right, then left, opposite of the pedal stroke
- your weight is over the bottom bracket
- you can feel the nose of the seat touching the back of your shorts
- you pull up and push the pedals forward with your feet
- you feel as if you are almost dancing on the pedals
- your whole body feels like one smooth machine

WHEN DESCENDING

- you are tucking your upper body
- keep your legs loose and moving
- look ahead
- drink, eat, plan ahead, especially on longer rides

TACTICALLY

- you are scanning the terrain and the pack, checking who is looking fresh, and calculating who is working hard and who is resting

- you select portions of the course to test yourself and others, such as accelerating out of a corner to see who is alert and who goes with you
- you get on the wheel of other riders moving up in order to maintain your position
- you are looking for opportunities to break away

WHEN SPRINTING

- you have selected a landmark at which point you will spring out of the saddle
- you are looking for that mark and the finish line, using your peripheral vision to monitor the racers around you
- you quietly shift into your sprinting gear and grip the handlebars tighter
- as you jump out of the saddle, all your energy is directed into pushing the pedals down as fast as you can
- you pull against the handlebars for more leverage
- as you get to top speed you ease yourself back into the saddle
- your pedal stroke becomes more round, and as fast as possible
- every pedal stroke counts, and you don't stop pedaling until you cross the line

For a two- or three-hour road race it is difficult, maybe impossible, to imagine the entire race. However, you can imagine parts of the race, especially the most difficult parts. You can imagine the challenging climb; breaking away;

attacking and jumping on a wheel; being crafty and pacing yourself wisely; positioning yourself for the group sprint at the end; and attacking, hammering and handling that situation effectively.

ON A MOUNTAIN BIKE

- you start your race sprinting to get a good position in the field
- once on the course, you focus on lowering your heart rate and recovering from the sprint effort, maintaining a pace that you'll be able to hold
- conserve enough to increase your effort in the last quarter of the race
- you scan the terrain and follow your plan of where to make an effort and where to ease up
- you use your hips to rebalance the body and bike over the bumps on the trail
- you use your arms and your weight to lift the front end of the bike, placing it over the obstacles
- lift the back of the bike with your feet and hips
- throw your hips forward to lunge the bike forward
- as your speed increases, you look farther ahead by standing on the pedals and letting the bike track itself
- breathe in and exhale, press your front wheel into the bottom of dips to clear the high side with ease
- lean the bike—not your body—and let it slide in certain places
- keep your weight back on decents

- use the front brake to control speed, back brake to control direction

ON THE TRACK

- focus completely on spinning the pedals as fast as possible
- feel the momentum of the fixed gear, pedaling slightly quicker with each stroke
- use the track's banking to push yourself as you come down
- always look ahead
- check under your elbow before moving up the track
- move up the banking to look down at the pack below
- again, focus like riding on the flats

VISUALIZE A CYCLING SKILL PRIOR TO PRACTICE.

HAVING A GOOD MENTAL IMAGE OF RIDING THE ROLLERS MAKES IT EASIER TO LEARN.

SCRIPTING

Chaining all these skills together, along with "smooth" and "attack" cues, can form a useful script of an upcoming event.

The following is an example of a script situation for a mountain-bike race:

- I'm warming up alone, feeling calm and focused.
- I have already checked in my equipment and have given my water bottles to the team manager.
- I'm breathing rhythmically, revving up the engine with my legs. Now it's time to go to the start line.
- I finish off my water bottle and take a full one to the start. I do deep breathing to relieve tension in the corral. I imagine myself racing a lap.
- Just before the gun goes off, I am alert. My crank is in position for the first power stroke; my elbows are bent, ready to place and pull the bike under me.
- Bang. We're off and I'm clicked in, standing on the pedals, sprinting and looking ahead. I sit down and continue the charge. We're in single track now.
- I begin to breathe deeply to slow my heart rate and recover from the starting effort. I'm relaxing, sitting up tall to breathe.
- I am finding a rhythm, using the riders in front of me for pacing.
- I climb seated, standing on steeper sections; I pump my bike over bumps and rocks. This is fun. I love this.
- One more long climb. I can do it.
- I shift gently for the descent, relax, and let the bike go, letting the front wheel track itself. I stand up and use my

hips to rebalance my bike and body over rough spots.

- In fast sections I look farther ahead. I push into the base of bumps and float over the top.
- I've completed one lap, and I'm going to smoothly ride out the second lap, paying attention to drinking and, perhaps, eating.
- At the end of lap two I want to be no more than 5 percent slower than the first lap.
- I want to hold that pace.
- In lap three, I focus even more on the task as I become tired. Breathing and recharging, I begin to pass others.
- I use the front brakes to control speed and the back brakes to control direction.
- In lap four I give all my effort on the sections I am good at. I'm very alert on those that I have difficulty with.
- I remind myself to breathe, use cue words and love the moment.
- I give an extra effort to pass others while looking like I'm riding with ease.
- I'm aware of my position and can pick off spots or pick up time with each pedal stroke. I'm reeling them in.
- As I cross the finish line I know I gave my best effort.

EXERCISE NO. 4: MAKING A SCRIPT

Chain together power words, thoughts, affirmations, images and skills to form your own script. First, select a course or event that you want to mentally prepare for. Select the desired feelings, power words, thoughts and affirmations that help you to perform well. Select the skills that the course demands and tactics that you think will improve your chances of having a good ride. As you trace the course, match the skills and thoughts you'll need in each section. Now, review the script you have created, adding thoughts that relate to when to "smooth" and when to "attack." Imagine riding the course using all the cues and thoughts you have prepared.

JULI FURTADO, CHRISSY REDDEN, LESLEY TOMLINSON AND CHRISTINE PLATT (CLOCKWISE FROM TOP LEFT) REHEARSE THEIR SCRIPTS PRIOR TO THE START OF THE CROSS-COUNTRY MOUNTAIN-BIKE WORLD CHAMPIONSHIPS. ALL ARE TUNED IN TO THEIR MENTAL TELEVISIONS, BUT EACH ONE IS ON A DIFFERENT PERFORMANCE PROGRAM.

Imagery is like a motion picture, and you are the director of that mental movie. Watching your own high-performance movies will help you excel. Here are six tips that will enhance your mental rehearsal and help you to direct a high-quality experience:

1. Define what you want. Uncertainty leads to confusion and stress. One way to increase success and reduce stress is to create clear images of what you want to do and how you want to do it. Stay tuned into these images. It's like radar that helps a plane or ship to navigate in low visibility. In defining your ride, be specific. Script it. Write it down. Do some constructive daydreaming. Project or stream your energy into the images of what you want to create.

2. Relax, then imagine. Whenever possible, release and breath before putting your creative imagination to work for you. As you do, the quality of your images will become stronger, clearer and more positive. Just taking a moment or two to relax and breathe will make it easier for you to imagine yourself riding at your best. In cycling that may mean being faster, more powerful, riding with ease, making good reads, having great jump and finishing strong.

3. Stay positive. You will get more of what you imagine. Stay focused on the image of you at your best. The only value in running a negative thought or image, something that didn't work, is to determine what you can do to change it and enhance your cycling performance and pleasure. Once you are clear about that, mentally rehearse the positive.

4. Easy at first. As a general rule, it's best to move from what's easy to what is more challenging. This is true in mental as well as physical training. To begin, see and feel yourself riding the easier sections of your race or ride with confidence, ease and speed, then mentally rehearse the more challenging aspects of the ride.

5. Be dynamic and brief. Create imagery that is a dynamic movie not a snapshot. Most riders find their imagery works best if they imagine the ride from the perspective of the rider on the bicycle. Others have had success visualizing their performance as if they were a spectator watching themselves perform from afar.

Try both approaches and see what feels and works best. Whatever perspective you choose, keep it brief. Obviously, you don't have to imagine the whole two-hour ride. You can benefit more by imagining 5 to 10 second flashes of the start, a hill, a breakaway move or a sprint finish.

Exceptions to this rule are downhill mountain-bike racers, who should mentally rehearse the entire course. But even here they can be most effective imagining brief, key segments and then chaining them together.

6. Use all your senses. Make your mental rehearsal multisensory. Most people are strongly visual and many think imagery is simply visual. Cycling has very strong visual, tactile and kinesthetic elements. Incorporate all the sensory cues into your mental rehearsal. See it, feel it, hear it, and when appropriate, smell it and taste it.

PEG Movies are a great way to recharge motivation. Perhaps it's because they stimulate us completely: visually, aurally and emotionally. My Dad and I laughed when we saw an early morning jogger punching the air the day after Rocky was shown on television for the first time. Movies can pump you up. Three favorites movies that excite me about making the effort are *Dead Poets Society, Meatballs,* and of course *Breaking Away.* Check out your favorites again.

EXERCISE NO. 5: SENSORY IMAGING

Practice imaging with a common example. Imagine tasting a lemon. Try this exercise and observe your full reaction.

You walk into the kitchen and go to the refrigerator. You open the door. You look around and see a large ripe lemon, and you pick it up. It feels cool in the palm of your hand. You smell it. You pick up a knife and slice into the lemon. Then, you squeeze a couple of drops of lemon juice into your mouth. Instantly you can taste the lemon's sour juice flowing into your mouth, onto the back of your tongue.

Most people can certainly experience themselves salivating as they imagine tasting the lemon. Those who imagine with all senses can also recall hearing the refrigerator door crack open and feel its cold air as well as the coolness of the lemon, the lemon's smell, and the juice running down your arm. How thorough was your experience? You can enhance your imaging ability with practice.

PEG Sometimes when I want to relax and clear my mind, I imagine going to a favorite place that is peaceful and brings back positive memories. Once I visualized my favorite camping trip. I was proud of going alone and pitching my own tent. I recalled it in such detail that I could actually taste the black currant juice and the chocolate spice muffins I had for breakfast. I wouldn't have recalled that otherwise, but imaging let me re-experience the tastes, smells, sounds, sights and feel of camping.

Image of success

In addition to mental rehearsal, a second type of imagery that can be incorporated into your cycling is to think of the successful end result. Create and hold the image of exactly what it is that you are working toward.

Most sport psychologists would say that it is more important to think of the process of getting there than it is to think of the end result. I agree. However, clarifying intention with an image can mobilize a process that puts powerful unconscious forces to work for you. It can also sustain you and help you to endure the rigors of training necessary to get you where you want to go.

I remember hearing Yury Kashirin, Canada's head cycling coach, discuss training schedules with a group of competitive recreational riders in Vancouver, British Columbia. Yury told the group that to be internationally competitive a cyclist needed to have a training base of 30,000 kilometers per year. Several riders were shocked by the magnitude of the commitment. One rider asked, "Couldn't I compete if I rode 10,000 kilometers?" Yury looked at him very matter-of-factly and said, "No."

There are certain aerobic requirements to be an internationally competitive bicycle racer. That's just the way it is. One of the things that helps some riders leave their warm bed for a two-hour training ride in the cold, rain and dark is the image of that successful end result.

A successful goal image can energize and sustain a rider during the hundreds of training hours and thousands of kilometers necessary to be a competitive international cyclist. Visualizing yourself as part of the national team at the Olympics, seeing yourself on the winner's podium at the end of the race, seeing yourself smiling after successfully completing a century ride, seeing yourself riding the last leg of your triathlon in the lead group, having the speed and power to be passing people as you finish a race, or having the energy to enjoy a cycling camping trip are images that may help you to sustain the drive to get you where you want to go. Putting a photograph up on your wall of you on the winner's podium, crossing the finish line, or riding through beautiful countryside may also help you get to where you want to go.

The successful image is no substitute for the pure enjoyment of riding—the feeling of speed, the wind, the companionship of other riders, or the plain and simple hard training necessary to be good. But it can sure help.

Exercise No. 6:
Imagine a successful end result

Pick an end result and put a picture or key word up on the wall that reminds you why the training you choose to do is important, and that it gives you the energy to maintain your efforts.

Stimulating images

The third kind of imagery that helps athletes excel, and one that some riders have found to be useful—and others have found to be fun—is to think of the question: "If you had to pick an animal, which one would give you qualities you want to have as you race or ride in order for you to be at your best?"

The animals that most riders select have been the big cats: cheetahs, leopards, jaguars, cougars, panthers and tigers. Some have picked eagles and wolves.

ROBERT MAJOR PHOTOS

IMAGINE SUCCESSFUL END RESULTS, SUCH AS THESE WORLD CUP WINS
FOR CADEL EVANS AND ALISON SYDOR.

The idea is that each of us is a combination of an angel—
a divine being that can create its reality—and an animal with
a strong, powerful physical body, emotions and feelings. As
angels we can use thoughts and images to shape our destiny.
We create and hold pictures of the future that become our
present reality.

Another part of us is that of an animal. That's what we are. We can use imagery to awaken the animal spirit that is within us. The thing about big cats is that they have tremendous power, balance and speed. They are brave and aggressive. They are crafty and smart. They love to hunt, and they never worry. If they return from hunting without any prey they don't worry about it. And, unlike some cyclists I have known, they don't run themselves down or get depressed.

By selecting the cheetah or the tiger you can identify with a power source that has great courage and heart, suprahuman quickness and speed, strength and power, and remarkable reflexes that can attack and hunt efficiently. Animal images can provide power and heart.

The animal image you choose should be used to represent you at your best. That is you at your physically strongest, with sharp reflexes, quick reactions, great balance, power and jump. When you say to yourself the word "cheetah," "tiger," "jaguar," or whatever your image is, allow it to awaken that animal in you; allow it to stimulate you to spin the wheel.

Spinning the wheel fires up the cheetah. It awakens your speed, jump and power.

One of the riders I worked with who used stimulating images successfully was Olympic silver medalist Brian Walton. Brian chose the image of a wolf. He liked the concept and the image. As a road racer and a pursuit rider, the wolf seemed to be the perfect image for him. He has to ride both in the pack and on his own, like a lone wolf. Brian found the wolf image so appealing and useful that he even tattooed the image of a wolf on his leg.

There are times, especially in a road race, when Brian described feeling tired, exhausted and alone. At such times he used his fatigue or angst to spin the wheel and fire up the wolf. It gave him energy. The wolf can run hundreds of miles on its own, and the wolf gains strength from the pack. Imagining the wolf spinning the wheel and generating power can sustain you on those long lonely moments of road racing, mountain biking, time trialing or pursuing. And it's fun. Try it. It's something that may give you power.

Steve, an Olympic medalist, invited me to Europe to work with him as he trained for the world championships. As a very successful international rider, he was living in Europe in rather comfortable accommodations, quite removed from the sparse and spartan circumstances that had nurtured his competitive spirit years before. He liked the image of a tiger and had used it in the past.

I suggested that he reawaken the image of the tiger to be competitive at the world championships. I reminded him how to use his breathing—to spin the wheel and fire up the tiger, then I suggested, half-jokingly, that in order to stimulate that animal quality in his life perhaps he should give up the soft life, the floral bed sheets, the waterbed and the rich desserts, and go out and sleep in the back yard to get himself ready.

If you are going to use animal imagery and call on the energy and spirit that's there...you have to do the training necessary to support it.

EXERCISE NO. 7: ANIMAL IMAGERY

Select the image of an animal that appeals to you. Think about turning the wheel, generating power and firing up the tiger, panther, cheetah or wolf. Think about spinning the wheel, generating power and sending it out into a five-pointed star.

Fire up the feeling you want to have. Think about power, attack or smooth. Think of the strategy you want to have, and think "eyes" or "tuck." Think about the tiger, panther, cheetah or wolf again.

Use the situation to generate power and introduce a thought, feeling or image that will give you the kind of effect you want to experience.

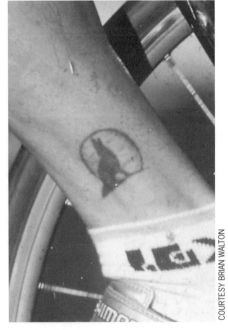

COURTESY BRIAN WALTON

PEG There are no limits to your creativity. Riders have used all kinds of stimulating images to enhance their performance: colors such as red jerseys that are waving in front of them, making them angry like a bull, and giving them energy to attack; sounds, like a race horse coming

BRIAN WALTON'S WOLF TATTOO.

out of the starting gate after the ringing of a bell; or use the sound of the crowd to exaggerate the importance of the moment, reminding yourself to spin the wheel and generate more energy; refueling, like Popeye getting energy from spinach.

The following is an example of imagery that Peg has used. This one gave her a warm feeling that helped her to set a world record, riding more than 490 miles in 24 hours.

PEG Before setting the world endurance record in Florida, I worked with a special massage therapist named Tom Hood. Tom was aware of my sport psychology skills and encouraged me to use them as he worked on my body, releasing over-worked muscles. One of the ideas I used was imagining the pros in the old days, when they wore red felt patches over their knees in cold weather to protect them. The felt was treated with warming salve and had adhesive, much like moleskin. When my knees were aching during the event, I imagined I had red felt on them, warming and protecting them. During one of the rest breaks, Tom checked me over, quickly pressing his hands over my body. He felt my knees and said, "You've been working on your knees, haven't you?" He could actually feel a temperature difference in them. My knees were warmer from imagining the red felt on them and they didn't bother me any more.

I ran an interdisciplinary pain clinic for six years treating many people with intense, long-standing pain. One of the most helpful tools we used to deal with their pain was imagery. Imagining warm hands, for example, has helped many people reduce the discomfort of headaches. Peg's example illustrates how one can use creative imagery to reduce pain and increase performance. Another of Peg's examples is an illustration of how to use imagery to lighten up.

PEG Another example that I love to recall comes from spring training in Arizona. On many mornings we saw hot air balloons ascend over the desert. I loved the bright colors and the way they floated so effortlessly. If we were close, we could actually hear the hot air blasts filling the cloth and slowly taking the basket up higher and higher. I heard that the participants' picnics were very decadent, with champagne served airborne.

Imagining being in a balloon or being a balloon still gives me a great sense of ease, lightness and fun. It slows time down and builds energy, like the hot air filling the balloon cloth. It helps me start the day of racing or training with a sense of wonder, letting the wind guide me. It helps me to leave the fear and need to control behind, far away on the earth.

Peg's third example illustrates how you can use the images or attributes of others to enhance your performance.

PEG In the difficult Elkhorn circuit stage of the old Ore-Ida (now the Hewlett-Packard Women's Challenge), I was struggling toward the back of the pack up the climb when I heard Marianne Berglund's support person call to her, "Marianne, you're glowing." That also meant something to me, and I was energized by the idea, imagining glowing like a hot ember, a hot rider. It helped me to move up and sit higher up in the pack.

Flashback

The focus of this session is to bring cycling-enhancing

imagery to the feelings we discussed earlier. In chapters one and two we discussed feelings. We described the breath as waves in the ocean, and creating a smooth flow as you ride. In chapter two we talked about spinning the wheel, generating power, and sending it out and about using the situation—such as fatigue, the incline or the sprint—as a stimulus to turn the wheel, generate power and move forward.

In chapter three we introduced the use of power words to enhance cycling. Here, in chapter four we presented some suggestions on how you can use imagery for optimal cycling.

HOMEWORK

Practice is essential to incorporate the imagery suggestions offered in this chapter. There are five homework assignments for the week.

1. The first assignment is to continue working with your breathing and relaxation on a daily basis, both on the bike and with a 10-minute relaxing breathing session every day.

2. Power words and thoughts:

A. Work with at least six power words this week. Select two of the feeling words you used last week, two strategy words, plus "attack" and "smooth." Combine them with your breathing. Incorporate them into your race training.

B. Continue to work with affirmations. Select six favorite power thoughts. Continue to repeat them several times a day, as you did last week.

Assignments three, four and five will use the three kinds of imagery discussed in this chapter: mental rehearsal, imaging the successful end result, and animal imagery.

3. Mental rehearsal. Create a script of a race course or ride you have experienced that is similar to a ride you anticipate doing in the near future. Imagine the course and write out a script. Then, mentally rehearse the elements of that script. As I said in this chapter, mentally rehearsing the course is extremely important preparation, especially if you are a mountain biker.

Visualize yourself being "smooth" as you expertly handle going through the difficult sections of the course. Imagine yourself with good acceleration in the speed zones. See yourself in control, being the boss, eyes open, making good decisions, anticipating and executing well.

Mental rehearsal can also be useful for a track racer. Trackies may have a clearer program or pattern of their race and it would be helpful to use mental rehearsal both to improve anticipation and reaction, as well as overall technique and form. One way to work on managing your mind is to script a proposed ride or race and then mentally rehearse yourself riding the course with speed, power and control (see exercise No. 2).

4. Select the image of a successful end result—something that you want to experience or achieve. It is important to have a picture of what you are striving for. Put a representation—picture or drawing—of that image up on your wall or somewhere in front of you, where you can see it. Put that image in your mind. Clarifying intention is very empowering. Projecting and reflecting on that image can give you support and energy to carry on and to realize your goal or dream.

Every once in a while sit back and imagine having achieved that goal. It's been said that what the mind can conceive and believe, it can achieve. Feel it, see it, believe it and do it.

5. Animal imagery: Finally, think of an animal that gives you the qualities that you would like to bring to your ride. Pick an animal that appeals to you and that you find stimulating. The big cats are popular because of their speed, balance, quickness, strength and beauty. Wolves are popular because of their ability to run alone for long distances, as well as their ability to hunt and run in the pack. Allow yourself to experience an awakening of your animal instinct. It can stimulate your cycling and provide a rich power source to be tapped. Work hard and have fun.

SPOT CHECK: SHIPPING YOUR BIKE

At some point you may be traveling to a cycling event. Here is some practical advice on how to carefully pack and travel with your bike.

PEG There are many options for traveling with your bike. It can be shipped ahead by bus or courier. When you fly, most airlines accept bikes for an excessive fee that should include a seat, meal and mileage points. There are many bike-packing options ranging from hard-covered cases, soft-sided bags on wheels, cardboard bike boxes, to airline-provided plastic bags. In most cases, some disassembling of the bike is necessary. Remove skewers from wheels and pad all parts and tubes of the bike frame. Pipe insulation from a plumber's supply store works very well for protecting the tubes. Secure the padding with duct tape. Protect the forks and dropouts from being crushed by inserting old hubs with skewers in the frame. Some travel cases come with those braces built into the floor of the case. If you travel frequently, try to remove as few parts as possible. The constant removing and replacing wears out threads, and you may find yourself having to seek out a shop that can retap the threads of your derailleur hanger, crank arm, pedal or stem bolt. I have never found it necessary to let air out of the tires before flying.

Always carry on your cycling shoes and racing clothes. It is easier to find a replacement bike, helmet and gloves, but replacing cleated shoes and clothing is not easy. Remove and carry on any parts that are unique and difficult to replace. Too often, bikes don't arrive, are damaged or "go missing." Check your bike before you leave the luggage claim area. Keep a record of your bike—the identifying serial number is stamped under the bottom bracket—note model name, model number, brand and make of components, wheels and tires. Most importantly, have a diagram of your bike position including seat height, dimensions of the frame—length of the tubes and angles between tubes—distance from nose of seat to handlebars, stem length and height, and seat set-back measuring the distance of the nose of the seat in relation to the center of the bottom bracket, measured by dropping a plumb line from the nose of the seat. With these dimensions it is much easier to recreate your position on another bike.

Find a good insurance company that covers bikes, or create your own "bike insurance" account. Before flying to a foreign country, obtain a bike registration form. This identifies the bike as yours, so you won't be suspected of purchasing the bike abroad and evading duty fees.

On that fatal day that your bike doesn't arrive, don't despair. Remember you have choices about how to respond. My bike didn't arrive once when I had a short reprieve at home. And I was really upset when it didn't arrive the next day, either. I went for a walk to try to calm down. During the walk, I imagined writing down these wasted days in my training diary. Then I saw myself flipping through the pages, day after day, week after week of rides and races. I realized that these days would be insignificant when looking back on the year as a whole. I came back from the walk more relaxed and actually looking forward to doing some other activities I liked to do. I had no control over the situation and chose to let it go and focus on what I could change—my attitude and my activities. The bike did eventually turn up.

Another time, I flew to a race and began to put my bike together at the hotel. Guess what? I hadn't packed my front wheel! I didn't panic. I knew which friendly race crew to call and borrowed a wheel for the race.

I have seen riders have to borrow bikes to train while awaiting their's "lost in transit" prior to a major international event. Don't compound things by creating upset. Remember—after studying chapters one through five—you are a master of emotional control. Even if you are feeling anxious waiting for the mechanic who is at the airport picking up and assembling your bike minutes before the race, "use it." Some riders have ridden their best races when things like this happened to them.

HOMEWORK REVIEW

During our weekly session in Vancouver, the following question came up from one of the eight riders.

ATHLETE Can we use breathing for recovery and also to get up for a race?

PEG You can use breathing to calm down and smooth things out on and off the bike. From a recovery point of view, you can use breathing for deep relaxation, drawing in energy and sending it out through the body (the five-pointed star) to recharge. You can use it when you are working with a massage therapist, or when stretching, to get a better quality stretch and send more oxygen into the muscles and tissues you are focusing on. In the latter case, it will allow you to go deeper into sore spots and facilitate healing and recovery. It can also help you bring more ease to the moment and make better use of your rest time, as well as help you get to sleep more easily, and tune a nervous mind away from a preoccupation with training and racing. To get up for a race, experiment with breathing in two ways. First, sit back, relax and breathe, and actively imagine riding with speed, ease and power. Second, to pump up, experience yourself spinning the wheel, breathing deeper and more forcefully, then pair that charged breathing with power words and power imagery— such as a panther hunting, pistons driving or a steam engine accelerating.

More homework feedback

PEG The riders liked the idea of imagining they were someone else, taking on the attribute of a better climber or sprinter. I shared with them how I sometimes run Phil Liggett, the Tour de France announcer's commentary through my head. Phil scripts the race for me, and I listen to it unfolding, getting excited and motivated by the images instead of listening to my negative thoughts.

We also talked about how hard a rider has to push to make an attack become a winning move. Most people experienced fear about that pain, or backed off from the pain if someone else made them hurt. All felt that the techniques in this session could help them to face fear and prepare for pain, by imagining a positive end result. A comment was made that "you know you are doing it right when you are pushing into the pain, and going beyond it."

Then, we played with stimulating images. It was almost like holding up flash cards. I suggested an animal or racing machine while they were imagining races. Some riders were stimulated by big cat images; for others it was Formula One cars, motorcycles or jets. It was a good way to explore what worked for us and what didn't. Everyone is different.

ATHLETE I have asthma and could feel how tight my breathing was on the warm-up. Normally, I don't like to think about that.

PEG It does help to think about difficult times in races if you continue to visualize solutions. Go back to the difficult situation again, and practice deep breathing and riding through the stressful moment, and doing it better than before.

CHAPTER FIVE

An optimal *cycling attitude*

"Attitude is a matter of choice."
—Dr. Miller

"Some riders with identity get nicknames like the Badger, Professor, Thor, Cheetah and the Blade.
And then there's the rest of the pack."
—Peg

The goal of chapter five is to review some of the elements that go into creating an optimal cycling attitude, and to encourage you to refocus on commitment, confidence and identity issues in your cycling career.

In the last two chapters we talked about focus and "power programs." These are the power words and power images that you can use to enhance your energy level, emotion and direction to perform at your best.

In chapter one we said that each of us has a personal connection to an unlimited supply of energy. With each breath you can tap that supply. Thoughts and images are also energy. You have a personal connection to an unlimited source of power words and high performance images from which to choose in order to enhance your performance and well being. Remember, you are the boss. Take a breath. Tune into thoughts and images that empower you.

THE ULTIMATE POWER WORD

Now, we will add a power word to the list of suggestions that you received in chapter three. Try to use this word and see if, and how, it can be useful for you. The new power word is LOVE.

Love is an antidote to fear. Fear is the greatest limiting program that people run on their mental TVs. Fear has many faces. It can be fear of failure, fear of not meeting expectations, fear of letting the team down, fear of embarrassment, fear of getting hurt, fear of losing control, and fear of the unknown. As we have said many times, fear causes tension and contraction. It cuts down breathing, reduces energy flow, and it reduces performance.

Love is more powerful than fear. While fear can motivate a good performance, love can inspire the great performance.

As human beings, love and creative thought are two of the greatest forces available to us. When we combine them with training, remarkable things are possible.

Love + creative thought + training = remarkable performance

Interesting? Perhaps. But how does this relate to cycling? Imagine yourself going into a race. The competition consists of some of the best riders around. Imagine feeling anxious, even fearful. Imagine wondering, "Can I really compete with these people?" Imagine running negative and fearful thoughts, "I don't want to be embarrassed. I don't want to look bad."

Awareness is the first step to managing your mind. To effect change you must first be aware of what you are thinking. And, if what you are thinking or imagining doesn't feel good to you, change the channel. "Use it." Use fear and negativity as reminders to go back into your breathing, spin the wheel and introduce a more positive, loving, empowering program.

Choose something to love in the situation.

Before a challenging race you may think, "I love the challenge," "I love feeling healthy," "I love to ride" or "I love to compete."

Love produces ease. Fear produces dis-ease.

To make the most of any situation you're facing, even a challenging situation, choose it, use it, love it and transform it.

Remember, you always have a choice as to whether you love or fear. Choose to bring love to the race situation. Choose to bring love to your training. Love feels good, and it's empowering.

EXERCISE NO. 1: LOVE CYCLING

Think of some of the race imagery we discussed in the last session. Envision shifting gears quickly, assessing situations well, and shifting from "attack" to "smooth." In some races negotiating the "smooth situations" can be very difficult and frightening. Again, think to yourself, "I love the challenge," "I love to handle the bike through difficult terrain," "I love being out there on the edge," and "I love pushing the envelope." Thinking "love thoughts" can change your feelings and make handling those challenging situations easier.

Love produces ease.

Fear produces dis-ease.

It's your choice.

You're the boss.

Love thoughts help you to tap a limitless power source. People can ride a good race with fear. Imagine a bear chasing you through the woods. You are racing ahead of it, and you are frightened and tense. You are trying to escape quickly. Fear stimulates action. But the greatest races come when people go beyond fear and move into love. The winners love to ride, and love the challenge. They love being there, and love to compete. They love quality competition. They love pushing themselves into the unknown. Even if they aren't successful, not meeting a race goal can be seen as an opportunity to love themselves and the event.

Cycling is a mirror. It's an opportunity to learn and to grow, to discover what you have to work on to become a better cyclist and to empower yourself.

Many people use fear of failure to push themselves to succeed. They run themselves down if and when they don't perform well. Go beyond making cycling a negative driver. Think to yourself, "As much as I want to succeed, I don't need to achieve something in order to be something. I'm okay."

Choose to be a lover.

Find something to love in every cycling situation. If it sounds challenging, begin by acknowledging yourself first.

The two most basic ways to love yourself are:

• giving yourself time to breathe smoothly and easily, and

• saying positive, loving things to yourself.

Love yourself. Take time to breathe, to draw in energy. It's there for you. Inspire yourself.

Love yourself. Look for and acknowledge the positive of who you are. Love your courage, love your discipline, and love your commitment to compete and to grow. Love the feedback and the honesty of the process.

Realize that you are a human being, not a human doing.

Envision yourself "being" with ease and power. Explore how you can use love as a power word in your racing next week. See how it feels, and love the challenge of that.

Continue working with your power words. Keep using them because repetition builds strength. If a couple of words don't feel right to you, let them go. For example, if the word "crafty" makes you feel sneaky instead of inspiring alertness, don't use it. If you don't like "boss" because you associate it with being bossy rather than being in control, find another power word. Always be looking for new words. Add a new word or drop a word that you're not using, or one that doesn't seem to have power for you.

Love is powerful. Be a lover.

Find things to love about what you do.

A NEW POWER IMAGE

I would like to add a new image to the imagery suggestions made in the last chapter. This new image is a combination of mental rehearsal and a stimulating imagery. It's something that I've used with a number of bike racers over the years, including one rider who was a three-time Olympic medalist and a world record holder.

Here's the idea. Two things that you may be aware of are:

• Our physical body is surrounded by an energy aura. This aura is not seen by most people. However, some people report being able to see auras.

• The second thing that you know as a rider is that when you are drafting off someone or something in front of you, whether it's another rider, a car or a pacing motor bike, you can reduce your energy expenditure by 20 to 30 percent. The reason is that the wind resistance you encounter as a rider is reduced by being sheltered.

Okay, now here's a question for you. If you are in a bike-riding situation and there is no one in front of you to draft off, is there anything—other then assuming good aerodynamic position on the bicycle—that you could do to reduce the wind resistance? Is there any way you could use imagery to reduce the resistance you experience?

Think about it.

Let's push the envelope on the creative use of imagery.

What if you could imagine an energy aura around you, and, if you could, shape it with imagery into a streamlined knife form around you. Could that knife-point reduce wind resistance, making you more aerodynamic and streamlined? Would it reduce the drag as well as your energy expenditure, and enable you to go faster?

I've introduced this concept to a number of racers. Some have found it very appealing, including the world sprint record holder. Others have found it too "far out"—something they didn't feel comfortable incorporating into their race programming, so they didn't use it.

I present the image for two reasons. First, I think it has validity. In certain race situations that demand pure speed, the knife image can be useful. Try it. Try

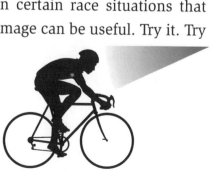

sending energy out in front of you as if you were pointing a knife straight ahead. Imagine cutting through wind resistance, and reducing drag and going faster longer.

Second, there are no rules. The greatest limits are those we impose upon ourselves with our thinking and attitudes. The knife image is an example of how you can use your creativity and energy to get more of what you want in your cycling performance.

Cycling is metaphoric of life. In this instance, it affords you an illustration of how to use imagery or thoughts in your life to create the experiences and results you desire.

EXERCISE NO. 2: KNIFING IMAGERY

To use the knife-energy image tune into your breathing. As always, pick up your breathing rhythm. Feel yourself draw in energy, and as you exhale think of sending energy up and out, the same way you did in thinking about "reeling in" riders ahead of you on the course. However, instead of sending energy and intention way down the road, this time simply think or imagine that you are shaping that aura in front of you.

Imagine riding your bicycle, and riding it very fast. You are out of the saddle with hips up and head pointed forward.

Now imagine sending your energy up and out in front of you, like a knife, stream-lining yourself. Imagine slicing through the wind resistance. Wind is flowing on either side of the knife's edge, and you are getting a drafting effect off your own image. You are feeling light and fast.

Experience the knifing imagery before you go out on the bicycle. Then, go out to ride some intervals. As you sprint, work at creating the knife image. Allow yourself to experience the effect of less resistance and more speed.

After a number of repetitions, and as you get a feel for that

TRY USING THE KNIFING IMAGE IN A TIME TRIAL,
LIKE THIS RIDER ON THE STARTING RAMP.

imagery, use it in more challenging competitive situations.

Bring "love" and the knife image to your cycling. The process of adding to, editing and developing your power programs never ends.

AN OPTIMAL CYCLING ATTITUDE

Now let's move on to another psychological aspect of optimal cycling: attitude. An attitude is a predisposition to respond. And a winning attitude is a predisposition to respond that moves you to being successful. There are several elements that make up a winning attitude for cycling, including:

- commitment
- identity
- confidence

119

Commitment

Commitment is the willingness to do what's necessary to get the result you want. It is a reflection of your motivation. Many people say "this is what I want" and set goals for themselves. There's no question that goalsetting is a basic expression of motivation and a key to success. As we said earlier, to be successful it's advisable to define clear, concise cycling goals: both long- and short-term. You should define a goal(s) as to what you want to accomplish on each training session or ride. Goalsetting is an important beginning to being able to focus your energies. However, most of us know that setting goals doesn't automatically guarantee success. Many people are simply not willing to do the day-to-day work necessary to make their goals happen.

In discussing successful end-result images, I said it's important to have clear intention. In order to manifest success you must support your intention with action in the form of day-to-day training. If your goal is to get to the top of the mountain, the way up is one step at a time. In cycling, one step at a time means doing the day-to-day physical and mental training necessary to build up the strength, aerobic capacity, technical skill and race understanding necessary to excel.

WILLINGNESS TO DO WHAT'S NECESSARY

One of the keys to optimal cycling is this willingness to do what's necessary in terms of the time, miles, effort and acquired race experience to be able to excel.

From a mental training point of view it goes back to a principle that we discussed in chapter one. Whatever comes up, "use it." Either you use it, or it uses you. Indeed, if your commitment is genuine, then your only choice is to use it.

Commitment is always about using it. If you are genuinely committed to moving forward, then you are inclined and obliged to use whatever challenge or obstacle is in front of you. The question becomes, "How?"

The answer always begins with the psycho-physical. When confronted with stress and adversity, most people psycho-physically tense up. They react with a natural defensiveness. They contract. When they contract they inhibit their breathing, reduce their energy and tune-in to defensive and limiting programs. Though they may try to excel, performance is adversely affected.

Commitment is about seeing the contraction, even in the face of adversity, and using that awareness to go deeper into turning the wheel, generating power and refocusing or redirecting your energies to the positive elements that will empower you to be successful in cycling—and in life.

Commitment is being willing to do what's necessary. It's "using it" consciously and consistently in every situation.

Winners are not free from fear and negativity; they experience uncertainty and doubt. It's just that they don't dwell on it. They "use it" to refocus and stay on the power channel.

Here are two examples of helping cyclists to "use it."

Jay was a road racer and a worrier. He spent a lot of time thinking about his next race, and too frequently he thought about what could go wrong. When I began to counsel Jay, we started with relaxation and breathing. Then I asked Jay about his strengths and weaknesses. He described his "nervousness" as a weakness that he thought was affecting his cycling and stopping him from being consistent.

I encouraged Jay to do some "reframing." Instead of thinking about his nervousness as a liability, I suggested he appreciate it as a sensitivity and an intelligence. I explained to him that it could be a strength if he could "use it." When he felt anxious I reminded him to breathe and run a positive thought.

When Jay "got" that his nervousness wasn't all negative, but rather had the potential to become a strength, there was a marked shift in his behavior. Almost overnight he became a more positive person. Instead of responding to suggestions with "yeah, but..." he began to be affirmative and say "I've got an edge." And he believed it. When he felt the pressure, he began to ask himself "how can I use it?" Interestingly, two other things accompanied Jay's attitude shift. He appeared to be less anxious, and his racing became more rewarding.

Curt was a young kilo' racer and an Olympic medalist. I had known him for three years during which time we had done some cycle-psyching. We were sitting at the velodrome in Indianapolis, Indiana, before a major North American competition. It was a quiet moment and we were relaxed. I remember us looking at some clouds building in the north and trying to get a read on the weather, which seemed to be changing and might affect the race scheduled for that evening.

As we sat there quietly, a bird flew over and shit on Curt's leg. It was the kind of thing that simply couldn't go unnoticed.

I remember us looking at each other and smiling, then

saying to Curt, "You know, that's an omen."

"Really?" he asked skeptically.

"Definitely," I replied. "If a bird shits on your leg, it's a track record. And if a bird shits on your head, it's a world record."

Curt laughed. He was a positive-thinking athlete, and I wanted to ensure that he framed this meaningless happening in a positive way. Later that evening, he set a track record.

Modeling is one of the most powerful forms of learning. Coaches often present their athletes with positive examples that inspire motivation and enhance performance. Coach yourself. Look for examples of what you want to create from models around you. As you become more conscious of what's happening around you, choose to "use it."

EXERCISE NO. 3: REFRAMING

Think of some traits of yours that you have considered negative. Find something positive about those traits as in the above examples and script how you can "use it" in a more productive way. This is called "reframing."

Dharma

Dharma is a Buddhist word. It means "path to self realization."

Cycling is a dharma.

Anything that we invest ourselves in fully, anything that challenges us to the maximum, anything that places obstacles in our path, anything that forces us to confront the essence of who we are and what we believe and that exposes us to our weaknesses and vulnerability can be a path to self discovery and self realization. Cycling can do and be that if you commit yourself to it.

At the national track cycling championships I ran into Ken, a veteran rider whom I had known for several years. When I asked him what was happening, he replied that he had opened up a new bike shop and that he was devoting a great deal of his time, energy and spirit to making it a success. He said it was doing really well, but it had taken a lot of work to get it off the ground.

When I asked him how his cycling was going, he replied, "Not so well. I haven't really been able to get out and train the way I should." I told him that was certainly understandable, given the commitment required to start a new business. I said, "You did what you had to do to make your business a success. You must be pleased."

He said he was pleased with the shop; however, he was disappointed with his cycling performance. Then he added, "The way things are going now, I think that next year I'll be able to commit more time to training, and I'm sure if I do I'll be back."

Commitment is about priority and values. It is a key to becoming an optimal cyclist, or a success in any endeavor.

Identity

A second quality of winning attitude is identity. Your identity is who you, and to a lesser extent who others, perceive you to be. For most of us, identity evolves with time and life experiences. Most competitive cyclists identify themselves as a rider and racer. Your cycling identity can be a determinant of how you behave and perform as a cyclist.

It's been said that you get more of what you think about. And if you think you can do something, you may. If you think you can't, you won't.

Your cycling identity can give you the energy and confidence that will encourage you to excel, or it can act like a weight to slow you down, tire you, and limit you from expressing your potential.

Let me give you a couple of examples of the power of identity. In the late 1980s, when I was working with the Canadian Olympic cycling team, one of the road racers, Gervais, told me the story of a race he rode in Tennessee with the legendary Greg LeMond. LeMond was the first American to win the world's most prestigious and demanding cycling race—the Tour de France—and he did it three times.

Shortly after LeMond won the Tour de France for the first time, he was hunting with his brother-in-law in California when he was accidentally shot at close range with a shot-gun blast. More than 30 pellets entered his body. A 20-something-hour surgery saved his life, but several pellets, including one in the lining of his heart, could not be removed.

LeMond pulled through this terrible ordeal. And after a lengthy rehabilitation he began to race again. One of the first competitive races he entered following the shooting was the race in Tennessee. Gervais described LeMond as looking poorly, bringing truth to the rumors that he had just endured a near-death experience. He clearly did not look like the man who had won the Tour de France. Yet, when a small group of riders broke away from the field, LeMond was in that break-away group.

I asked Gervais and his teammates how was it that LeMond was in the breakaway group, considering he didn't look well and did not have the training consistency of the other riders. The only response they could think of, and it is one that often applies to the injured athlete, was "That's where he thought he belonged. That's who he thought he was."

That identity image of "who I am" and "where I belong" can move an athlete to do things that he or she thinks is phys-ically impossible. Conversely, wearing the identity or self-image of "a loser" or "choke" can be extremely limiting.

PEG Here is an example of identity, confidence and imagery.

Indeed, identity, confidence and self-image are inextrica-bly intertwined.

I was competing in a stage race in Colorado two weeks before the Olympic Trials. The course was very technical with narrow roads, many ups and downs, and lots of twists and turns. We were to race a road race on it later that day, but began by completing one lap solo, as a timed prologue to the stage race. After reviewing the course, I did not feel as confi-dent as I would have liked. I kept thinking "This is not my kind of course. It's not me."

I thought about how well one of my teammates could climb the early hilly sections, and how another would dive through the descents and corners in the middle section, and still anoth-er had a great pursuing sprint for the final flat kilometer. As I imagined their strengths, I stopped focusing on my own self-doubt. Something shifted and I began to feel more positive. I took on those attributes and attitudes of my teammates during the race. Much to everyone's surprise, I won the time trial. Later, I said it was due to great teamwork.

Our identity can lift us to super performances or slow us down and limit us. We tend to see our identity as who we are; however, it is not a static entity. Identity is something that has been formed over time, by experience, and it can be reshaped. You can change your mind.

Identity has much in common with confidence. Confidence also has to do with how

ROBERT MAJOR

ALISON SYDOR HAS THE IDENTITY OF BEING No. 1 ON THE WORLD CUP CIRCUIT. HERE SHE IS WEARING THE NUMBER ONE, OUT FRONT ALONE, WINNING BY A LARGE MARGIN.

we see ourselves. If someone is confident, they believe they can do the job, and that makes doing the job more probable. For most competitive cyclists the really important questions are: How do I grow my confidence? How do I transform doubt and negativity into the sense of being a winner?

The most basic ways to build confidence are by experiencing success and effective preparation. Return to the image of climbing the mountain. Break it down into stages and steps, with many steps constituting a stage. Set small goals. See yourself doing what's necessary, and taking the steps to ascend stage one, then move on to stage two, doing what's necessary and taking those steps. See yourself climbing the steps—small steps—doing the basics and performing them well at each step. As you do, your belief in your own ability will grow. Do it first with imagery, then in training, then make it happen in race situations.

To prepare for a mountain-bike race, break the challenge down into handling the difficult sections of the race first. Work on each section with physical and mental rehearsal until you think, "I can handle this part." Then move on to practice the next challenging part of the course. Work consistently with focus, feeling and commitment until, gradually, you have the sense of "I can do it. I can descend through this rocky part here, and I can handle a similar section over there." Then move on to the next challenge on the course. When you realize that you are not getting enough acceleration or jump into the speed areas, begin to work on that until your perception of the transition to speed is positive, which is to say that the image you have of yourself shifts and your confidence grows.

Gradually, chain together the elements you are mastering at each successful stage. As you do, your positive performance image and your confidence will improve. Gradually, you will sense and know that you have the attributes to handle the elements you may encounter in this stage, in this race and in other races. Eventually, you will look at a race course and say, "Yeah, I can handle it."

People sometimes become anxious when they find themselves facing a daunting, seemingly mountainous task. Well, remember the way up the mountain is one step and one stage at a time.

At a developmental training camp, one rider, a bike courier who was attempting to become a road racer, expressed some anxiety about the distance (160 kilometers) of an upcoming road race. "I don't know if I can make it," she said with a nervous smile. To make her challenge more palatable and the goal more achievable, I suggested she reduce the size of the challenge in her mind by breaking the race in to three stages.

One: "At the start, just think of riding a good 50k race. Get off to a good start, have good form, use your breathing and make the effort to be near the front. Think of it as just a 50k race," I counselled. "You can handle it."

Two: After completing her 50km ride, I suggested that she focus on the next 50km. I encouraged her to ride smart, keep her eyes open, use her breathing, maintain good form and be aggressive. Remember to say to yourself, "It's just 50 kilometers. I've done that before and I can do it well."

Three: When that second 50km was completed, I told her to acknowledge her effort and refocus. "You are a tiger. You are riding well. Now is not the time to reduce effort, you are two-thirds there. This is just a 60k race home. You can do it. Turn the wheel, generate energy, be smooth, be focused, finish well."

The question "How do you eat an elephant?" is best answered, "One bite at a time." When you are faced with cycling challenges that seem too large and overwhelming, one approach is to reduce the challenge to bite-sized chunks...and chew them well.

PEG My first experience working with a psychologist was after several successive racing disappointments. I was very depressed. I chose to work with her only on my attitude toward climbing, a relatively small problem. She taught me to listen to my inner dialogue, and stop the negative thoughts. If I said to myself, "Oh, no. Here comes the hill. I hate this part. This is where I always get dropped," I was to replace it with at least neutral comments such as, "I know I can make it to the top."

The truth is I wasn't as bad a climber as I made myself out to be. So I worked at it. Once I had some success in controlling those negative thoughts on solo training rides, first on smaller climbs, then on bigger ones, everything seemed to get better.

As I began to feel better, my confidence began to grow, and I actually began to look forward to climbing opportunities.

On occasion, I have tried to change confidence by shifting perspectives of the challenges facing a rider or group of riders. At the Pan American Games in Venezuela several of Canada's male road racers were depressed and intimidated by the hilly road course. They knew that they could power on the flats, but they did not see themselves as strong climbers. They thought that the smaller, quicker South American riders would easily out-climb them and that they didn't stand much of a chance in their event.

What you think can affect how you perform. They acknowledged that they weren't confident, that the hills frightened them and that they would tense up as they approached each climb. I thought they needed to lighten up and that a little humor would be helpful. So, I asked them to see the hills as breasts, giant breasts, and to imagine themselves riding into the giant inviting breasts. The thought certainly loosened them up; it seemed to help them shift perspective, feel lighter and be more positive about the challenge they faced.

In sport, success always leads to greater challenges and more difficult competition.

As things progress you may find yourself in a national or international competition against very experienced riders. As you look at or think about them you may feel some anxiety. You may wonder if you can compete or if you've lost confidence.

A key is not to compare yourself to them. Instead of thinking about them, and putting them on your mental TV screen, stay with the task at hand. Tune into the image of you performing the elements of the race successfully, just as you have done repeatedly in your physical and mental training. In a sense, you are not competing against them. They are only there to challenge you to be at your best. Remember you are the boss. Focus on the positive elements.

Here is an example from Peg on "using difficulty" during the first stage of the Idaho Women's Challenge in 1989, Emmett to Boise.

PEG Emmett, Idaho, is a land of plenty: plenty of fruit trees and plenty of pollen. And that's not good news for allergy sufferers and asthmatics. All the racers got a big dose of the airborne allergens before climbing out of the valley and up old Freezeout Hill.

My asthma began kicking in on the climb, but I was familiar with wheezing up ascents, anyway. It was on the flatter sections afterward, the fragrant farm area to be exact, that the full-blown reaction set in. The wheezing didn't calm down like it normally does. It remained rapid and choked, which alarmed me. My airways were constricted—I simply couldn't breathe. Now I was getting panicky and reached for my inhaler in my jersey pocket. I fumbled around, and others could hear my rasping. Quietly my teammates surrounded me and one placed a hand on my back, reassuring, steering me straight while I drew on the inhaler. Having the help of my teammates made it seem less scary and isolating. I took deep, slow inhales, willing the reaction to ease. They stayed nearby as the pack rolled along. My breathing became easier, tensions released. I felt so happy to get through that and to be riding in the race again, supported by my team. I began to form a plan.

The stage finished up Bogus Basin Road, the beginning of a long climb. In the past, I had gotten boxed in and crossed the line in the bunch, never having launched a final sprint. This time, I focused on the last several miles. I was determined to be in the action, even though I thought it might require pulling at the front the last two miles to maintain position. I did end up at the front a good part of the way. I saw a rival team set up a leadout with half-a-mile to go, so I matched its pace. I didn't dare look around, just focused on the upcoming finish line, looking straight ahead.

I didn't even know my teammate Lisa was on my wheel, being led out by me. I jumped before the others and brought it home for the win. Wow, it was so great to be able to make a move after that awful asthma attack—and what a bonus, I won! There was one more surprise. Lisa stayed on my wheel during the sprint and took second place. We were one-two! Plus, the time bonus she got for the second-place finish gave her enough seconds to move into first place overall. She wore the leader's jersey from that day on. I'm not sure which of the feelings was the greatest, overcoming that difficulty, winning the race, or contributing to the team's success, but together it was an unbeatable day.

EXERCISE No. 4: IMPROVING SCRIPTS

Identify some parts of courses that intimidate you. Think about strategy and self-talk that will loosen you up and free you to perform better on those sections.

A key to confidence is preparation

The easiest answer to the question, "How do I build my confidence?" is simply, "Improve your preparation, and change your focus."

Magic happens when you set small incremental goals. Work consistently, run positive programs, mentally rehearse things, think power thoughts, keep moving forward, take steps, say positive things to yourself, and acknowledge yourself for achieving each stage. Then, move on to the next stage, chain stages, and think more positive self-talk and imagery.

If you experience a negative performance, use it. Think of what you can do to improve performance next time. Then continue to move forward, frame your efforts in a positive light as you feel your confidence grow as well as the identity of yourself as someone who can.

Gaining confidence is the same in any field. Padreweski, the great pianist, allegedly said, "If I don't practice one day, I know it. If I don't practice for two days the critics know it. If I don't practice for three days, the whole world knows it."

I spent several years working with the Los Angeles Rams of the National Football League. One of the pressure-jobs in football is being a field goal kicker. The kicker's performance can be affected by both pressure and confidence. One regular routine that the Rams kicker went though to build his confidence at each practice was to start kicking short field goals, first, from the 10-yard line. After two or three successful kicks in a row he would move back to the 15-yard line. And with more success to the 20, 25, 30…and so on. As he progressed though this regular practice routine, he strengthened his confidence as well as his identity of himself as a competent kicker.

We explore competence in the next session. But the point here is confidence. It comes from success. Do the work necessary to experience success with each step toward your ultimate goal, and your confidence will grow.

Growing your successes and therefore your confidence is directly related to improving the quality of your mental preparation.

As we said earlier, for too many athletes, how they feel about themselves and their general sense of well-being is determined by how they perform. If they do well, they feel good about themselves. If they perform poorly, they feel terrible and worthless.

It's normal for people who are highly motivated and who work very hard to achieve certain performance goals to be disappointed with a poor performance. However, it's important to remember that you are not a result. Your effort doesn't determine who you are. You are a human being, not a human doing.

Begin your self-talk by thinking, "I'm okay."

EXERCISE NO. 5: IDENTITY STATEMENTS

Write out an identity statement of who you are, or could be when you are at your best. Affirm all of your strengths and highlight your potential. If you could be and you haven't yet manifested this quality, incorporate it into your identity statement. Read this statement to yourself. Repeat it often. Let it become you.

Here is an example of an identity statement used by an experienced and successful mountain biker:

- *I am an outstanding cyclist. I am a star.*
- *I am strong and fast, and I read the course well.*
- *I am a great starter. At the start line, I rev up and know I will charge to the front.*
- *I see opportunities, and I attack quickly and with confidence.*
- *I am very strong. I am a super climber, and I have great jump.*
- *I use my breathing to turn the wheel.*
- *I can maneuver the bike anywhere.*
- *My strength and bike-handling skills give me many options on challenging terrain.*

- *I am well prepared, and I make good choices.*
- *l am smart and steady.*
- *I am in excellent shape and pace well.*
- *I am a mountain lion.*
- *I am quick, strong and powerful.*
- *I am intense and focused like a hungry lion on the prowl.*
- *I have clear eyes.*
- *I see opportunities and good lines.*
- *I am quick to attack and ride the edge.*
- *I smooth the obstacles, and I descend like a fast cat.*
- *I use my breathing to pump and smooth.*
- *I work hard to be prepared, and I prepare myself well.*
- *I do my best, and the mountain lion doesn't worry about things it can't control.*
- *I enjoy racing, and I am very good at it.*

Psychologists who offer I.Q. testing know that a low score doesn't necessarily mean a lack of ability. It simply means that you didn't perform well that day. When you perform poorly, don't lock onto that disappointing perception and keep rerunning it as an identity program of who you are. Instead, "use it," say to yourself "That's not who I am." Then imagine yourself riding with ease and power, performing well, and enjoying the ride. Acknowledge that performer as who you are. And then work toward making it a reality.

HOMEWORK

1. Find things to love. Use love as a power word in your training. Love is one of the most powerful forces you can have working for you. As we said, love is an antidote to fear. Love to ride. Love to climb. Love speed. Love to train. Love to compete. Love a challenge. Love the superior riders—and use them. Love the inferior riders. Love yourself. Don't force it. Allow yourself to be a lover.

2. Experiment with the image of "knifing" through resistance. First imagine the concept. Allow yourself to see it and feel it clearly. Then, work with it on the bicycle, especially during interval training and in sprint situations. Use knifing with your other high-performance images.

3. Explore your commitment. Set some goals. See yourself working toward them. Imagine obstacles. See yourself using adversity—fear, pain and difficulty. Winners use everything. One of the keys to commitment is learning how to use adversity.

4. Take a look at your identity and confidence. Think of your strengths as a rider, and fill in these blanks.

Write down "I am a good _____."

Consider the elements that make you good at your event, and note what you have to do to maintain your strengths.

Develop a training program with steps and stages that will help you maintain your competence at an event. As you work on your program, use positive self talk, power words and imagery. Strengthen your identity as someone who is good at _____.

Think of an area that you must improve as a rider.

Write down "I am improving my _____."

Consider the elements necessary for you to be a competent _____.

Note what you would have to do to improve in these

areas. Develop a training schedule with steps and stages to improve in this area.

As you work on your program use your positive self talk, power words and imagery.

Grow your identity as someone who is good at

_____.

Review and edit your identity statement (in exercise No. 5). Record your statement in your training journal. Several times a day read or repeat your identity statement. Make it a regular part of your training program.

SPOT CHECK: HEART RATE MONITOR USE

Cyclists use heart rate monitors to get more precise feedback about their performance. Heart rate is a measure of how hard the body is working. Instead of going simply by intuition or feel—"this effort feels hard enough"—the heart rate monitor provides an exact reading of exercise effort level. The exercise heart rate can be expressed as a percentage of the highest heart rate ever observed by the individual: 80 percent of maximum heart rate is 160 beats per minute for a person whose max is 200 bpm (80 percent = 160/200 x 100).

There are guidelines for percentage of heart rate training:

ZONE 1 up to 60 percent of maximum heart rate begins aerobic training

ZONE 2 60-80 percent develops strength and the cardiovascular energy system

ZONE 3 80-90 percent develops sub-maximal efforts

ZONE 4 90-100 percent works maximal and lactic acid-producing efforts

The heart rate monitor takes the guess work out of training by letting you know exactly in which zone you are training.

Using a heart rate monitor can facilitate staying focused. For example, if your attention drifts and if you slack off, you will clearly observe a drop in heart rate. If you haven't been training enough, the heart rate monitor will show you that you can't hold a high (zone 3 or 4) heart rate, and that your heart is slow to return to your resting level. When fatigued, you will notice that your heart rate will be higher than normal. The heart rate monitor prevents you from overtraining in that situation. If you stick to your prescribed heart rate zone in training that day, your effort level will have to be easier. Therefore, you won't be as likely to overdo it when you are too tired. Pushing yourself when you are too tired to get the benefit causes overtraining (see Spot Check, chapter six).

Recovery is another indicator that the heart rate monitor can measure. A rule of thumb is for a 30 beat drop in heart rate the minute after a maximal effort. Create a standard by checking yours one minute after a maximal effort. Compare this regularly to your norm. You may be overtired when your heart rate doesn't drop as quickly after hard efforts. The information provided by your heart rate monitor can be very useful to the sports physician when considering poor performance symptoms or assessing your overall health status and fitness level.

You can also use the heart rate monitor for feedback when pacing yourself. Some riders use the training and race strategy of keeping their heart rate above a predetermined rate. At a recent clinic, a rider shared that the first time she used a heart rate monitor in a race she was frightened by her readings because the numbers were so high. It's true that you will likely see higher heart rates in competition than in training. Emotions increase heart rate. Pushing also increases heart rate, as does increased body temperature and dehydration.

Use your heart rate information when planning race strategy. Remember, your heart rate will climb as you get tired or dehydrated, so if you are time trialing and you want to maintain speed, expect to experience increasing heart rate levels. The rider can plan what heart rate to work at during the race, and anticipate and manage an acceleration of heart rate later in the race. For example, a pursuit rider may know that they can hold their heart rate above 193 for the entire 4000 meters, so they will use 193 as a minimum, finishing at their max. Others use the information to hold back earlier in a race, saving more for the finish. Kirk Molday, winner of the 1997 NORBA National Championship Series, is an example of an athlete who starts out more slowly, holding back in the first half of a mountain-bike race by monitoring his heart rate. He increases his pace later, allowing his heart rate to climb, overtaking his opponents by the handful.

Use the heart rate monitor as a tool, along with your power programs and good form.

HOMEWORK REVIEW

Feedback from the riders at the sessions:

PEG Most riders are able to identify things they love about cycling. We discussed whether the things they love are highlighted in their training plans and goals. Some decided love was missing. Others realized the importance of incorporating the things they "love" into their preparation. For example, one loves to train alone and needed to schedule more of that. Another loves the group and needed to put more effort into attending workouts and organizing training partners. One needs to break monotony and cross-train with other activities such as hiking, camping or swimming for more balance and fun. Someone else wasn't being consistent enough to see improvement, something they love about training.

I remember the year that I took it relatively easy, just doing criteriums, not trying out for the world's team in any event. I had some new teammates, Sally and Sara. They used to rehash after the race, and I marveled at how much they simply enjoyed racing, how animated their reenactments were. It helped me to heal from placing too much pressure on myself, and expectations that were too high.

A few cyclists really liked the idea of "knifing." For most it was not fully developed yet and needed more time, like the spinning the wheel idea. One rider combined the aura idea with color, surrounding herself with red warmth or yellow electricity.

Commitment turned out to be an area of differing perspectives. For the athletes, it was a feeling of how important their cycling is to them. As a coach, I measured their commitment in terms of their actions, how often they showed up to workouts and the sport psychology sessions, if their bike was maintained, and if they wore proper clothing. The discussion showed us the importance of communication, of athletes giving the coach feedback on how their training is going and what else is happening in their lives. It's important that I follow through on requests for their training diaries to be completed and to find out how they are feeling—their perception of their performance. I can give them concrete measures of improvement. They can attach the emotional fulfillment.

Task four took a little prodding from the coach. Some athletes are reluctant to celebrate their strengths and their accomplishments. For those who completed this question, it was very rewarding and gave new focus to their preparation. It helped to individualize training for each rider. For example, one rider needed to improve his confidence in his cornering. He went out and practiced a challenging corner a dozen times and proved to himself that he can do it. It changed his self-talk from the negative "This is the worst" to "I'm okay."

One began a healthy questioning of why he should be doing speed work for an endurance event like Ironman. We discussed the benefits of doing longer intervals as opposed to the motivation he got from a training group that does speed work intervals that are too short for his event. Basically, what this session helped him with was broadening training from just a physical plan into one that includes skill competency and motivational rewards.

CHAPTER SIX

Competence
and
confidence

"*Imagine that you have been training for weeks, and one day you are out riding, doing the same thing you've been doing day after day. Let's say you are doing hill climbs with a big gear, and all of a sudden instead of straining and hurting, the killer climb feels almost easy and you realize that something good is happening. You are getting fitter and stronger. At that moment you can feel your confidence grow.*"

—Dr. Miller and Peg

"*Each time you ride your bike is an opportunity to feel better, to think positive thoughts about your cycling competency.*"

—Peg

The goal of chapter six is to define the elements required to be a competent cyclist in your discipline, and to underline that training and by developing specific competencies; to grow confidence.

This chapter reviews the three key areas to cycling competency: physical preparation, cycling skills and mental preparation. You train for physical preparation. In the process, you practice physical skills such as pedaling, shifting, cornering, climbing, sprinting and so on.... The physical and skill training also provides an opportunity to sharpen your mental skills. The three competencies work together, so with each ride you are increasing competency and confidence.

The first element of competency is being physically fit and that means physical training. Most riders appreciate that physical training is fundamental to optimal cycling. What is less often understood is, what is the right amount and mix of physical training? How much:

- aerobic training, which comes from riding for many hours and kilometers
- anaerobic training, usually in the form of interval training for building speed
- strength training, which comes from working with weights, plyometrics, medicine ball, machines and pulleys and using them specifically to build the muscles you need for your event
- cross-training such as running, swimming, skating and cross-country skiing in the off-season
- rest and regeneration

There are limitless combinations and variations of these elements. For example, using weights[7] then plyometrics, then intervals and motor-pacing to improve jump and sprinting. It takes time, diligence and good coaching to find the right combinations for each athlete.

It is also important to understand that doing the work—physically practicing these elements—can lead to the development of mental strengths such as awareness and confidence.

[7] see *Weight Training for Cyclists*, VeloPress, Boulder, CO, 1998.

For example, feeling stronger physically nurtures positive thinking and a positive identity. Showing up and putting in the work is discipline, another important mental strength. A rider's participation reflects their motivation, commitment, interest and available time. Appreciate your physical training.

PEG I was recently talking with an athlete who is very fit. She took a Conconi test in December that gave us the numbers to show her fitness level, and it was high. She has trained consistently with long rides, weights and one interval session per week. She is an upcoming downhill mountain-bike racer. Yet, when she was dropped from a pack in a group road ride on a four-minute climb, she determined that she was not fit at all. I said to her, "You are allowing one four-minute road climb that you will never encounter in a mountain-bike downhill event to change your whole outlook." When I framed that back to her, she could see what had happened. She regained perspective and refocused on what she is capable of doing well and is relevant to downhill racing. So, focus on your competencies, and say, "I can do this well."

Why is it that many cyclists train so much, but still don't feel confident? One way to conquer this feeling is to keep a log and document all of your training. Review it. It will show how much work you have put in. Sometimes, riders aren't sure if the training they are doing is correct. That is a question that requires some investigation.

While most cyclists train hard, they often don't make the connection between doing the physical training and using the experience gained from the training rides to build confidence.

They fail to recognize that their practice also works mental skills.

I asked a group of riders, "What is the value and purpose of your training? What does it mean that you can do seven hill repeats, or nine 1km intervals?"

Judging by the blank responses, they hadn't formed a clear connection between the physical training done in group workouts and confidence gained for an upcoming event. What is missing is understanding the specific elements that each event demands, doing that work, and then growing the confidence, knowing that "I'm prepared" and therefore "I can."

EXERCISE NO. 1:

IDENTIFY THE PHYSICAL TRAINING YOU NEED

1. Write down the event you are training for. You may want to use the "Cycling High Performance Athlete Profile" in Appendix B to help you decide the amount of aerobic, anaerobic, strength, power and endurance that the event demands. Seek help from more experienced cyclists and coaches.

2. Observe your competency in the physical traits identified.

SETTING GOALS

PEG I spent time with eight riders analyzing the physical demands of mountain-bike races, road races and track events. We discussed the importance of recovery from efforts, as well as endurance or leg speed. When you analyze your event this way it can become clearer to you what needs to be accomplished in order to be physically prepared. It can also highlight how your present training is actually improving the

APPRECIATE YOUR PHYSICAL TRAINING, LIKE
BEING ABLE TO CLIMB FASTER.

components needed to excel in your event. After developing this awareness, you will know which of those qualities you possess and which need more work. This process naturally leads us to goal-setting.

This method focuses the rider on What has to be done and generates goals based on "what should I improve?" rather than on successful end results such as making team X, beating Y or winning race Z.

For example, Tony aspired to be a top road racer. We knew that the national road course required endurance and great climbing ability. Tony's self-analysis was that he had natural speed, sprinted well and tended to be impatient during the first half of road races. Further, he was still recovering from being hit by a car last spring. Given these challenges, the goals Tony set for his preparation for the road race were to:

• rehabilitate his back

- build aerobic base for endurance
- improve climbing while seated, using bigger gears than before
- improve emotional control to save his energy for the second half of the race

All of these goals were behaviors that Tony had under his control. None of these goals involved making the national team. None have end results such as placings or beating a particular person. Tony could use those as measures, but he would also know if he is improving by:

- experiencing less or no back pain
- less fatigue on rides that are more than four hours— with no cramping, no need for a nap afterward, and faster average speed
- maintaining the same time on hill repeats while using a larger gear and a lower heart rate
- having more patience as reflected by fewer attacks and chase efforts in the first half of the race, as well as more significant ones in the last half

All of these items are measurable. Now, instead of saying, "I feel stronger," a rider can actually know why they are stronger, because "I can climb Cypress Mountain faster, in a bigger gear, with a lower heart rate" or "I can take longer pulls in the pace line while maintaining the group speed." As a coach, I can actually feel the relief—I can see it on a racer's face when they identify goals for improving, rather than placing. The pressure is reduced. And what pressure there is, is more intrinsic and is internally motivated. It's a joy to pursue these goals.

Now every time out on the bike, a rider can look for things

that improve his or her confidence. Things that let them say "This is what I need in my event" and "I can."

With this more objective method it's easier for cyclists to think about what events they are most naturally suited for. The road racer in the above example would make an excellent points racer. He has natural speed, is on top of every move, and always wins in sprints. He started training on the track in the winter and will try some track races in the spring. If he decides to stick to road racing, he will have the cross-training option of using the track for speed work. He will also benefit from the additional races, gaining race experience he missed last season due to the car accident.

EXERCISE NO. 2: GOAL-SETTING

Use the information about your strengths and weaknesses in Exercise No. 1 to set goals based on improving weaknesses. Set long-term or career goals first, then seasonal goals, monthly goals, weekly goals and daily goals. Use the short-term goals to lead you to the long-term success. For example, if your long-term goal is to get back your race fitness of several years ago, your monthly goals may be to increase volume, like riding more than two hours on Sundays in January, increasing to three hours by the end of February. Increasing the volume will help you to reach your season goal of being fit, having a good base, and performing well at a race in July. Remember to have goals of maintaining the traits you are already good at.

Physical training cannot be isolated from physical skills and mental training. Remember, as you train physically, you are displaying discipline, showing up, putting in the time and becoming stronger and more skilled. Riders can gain confidence from that.

PEG Again, a training diary is a visual way of recording that discipline. I tell riders that they get double points when they show up for training in the pouring rain, even if we wisely cut the ride short. They got themselves out and were ready to put in the training time. That tells me they are committed. Of course, it's more important that they tell themselves that they are committed, disciplined and physically prepared.

Sometimes the toughest part in training is just getting out the door when you don't feel like it. Most people feel better once they are out on the bike. If, after warming up, you still don't feel right, don't fight it and go back home. One of my first coaches had me add a preparation column to my training diary, to give myself credit for preparing well: pumping up my tires, bringing food and a jacket, having a workout plan.... This gave me positive feedback even on the days when I felt lousy and didn't complete the physical training.

Along with physical training, it's important to live a lifestyle that supports optimal cycling. We discuss lifestyle in the next chapter. Lifestyle nurtures training and performance. Lifestyle is a matter of choice.

PEG Here is an example of how your lifestyle needs to support your goals. Marion was a bright, talented rider who had a disappointing season. When we discussed what went wrong, she offered some ideas and added that she had just had "a lot of bad luck." To some extent, I believe we create our luck, and we do it with focus and preparation. In this rider's case, I recall seeing her at a manager's meeting at the national championships in an animated discussion about a variety of relevant issues just prior to her big race. These issues could have, and should have been, addressed by others, not by Marion, and not then, before her big race, shifting her focus and taking energy from that event. Another significant component to Marion's lack of luck was lifestyle. All season long, Marion never had a home base. She stayed with an assortment of friends. I believe that her transience affected her well-being and contributed to her "lack of luck."

CYCLING SKILL

What we are talking about is technique and skill in handling the bicycle as distinct from a level of fitness. For example, a very fit rider may be leading a race and lose it due to poor cornering or descending skills. There are specific skill sets required in each cycling specialty that you need in order to be competent enough to perform well in that event.

PEG Because we put so much emphasis on results, placings and who beat whom, we forget to look at how well we carved a turn, let go of the brakes, committed to a final sprint. These are the ideas in looking at our competency in the sport, appreciating how well we do the tasks as opposed to simply looking at the final result. The concept of competency awareness is increasingly being used in education and business in North America.

Dr. Susan Butt, a sport psychologist, has been a proponent of this idea for years. One country that embraces this focus on competency is Cuba, the country famous for producing

Olympic gold medalists in boxing. Dr. Butt says that part of training Cuba's boxers is getting them to think about an opponent as someone who can help them to improve their technique, who challenges their tactics and pushes them to a higher level, rather than as an object to destroy.

In our terminology, cyclists can "use" their opponents to stimulate performance in a similar way. Imagine your competitors as helping you to be your best, challenging you to push harder, corner faster, be more vigilant and stay calmer. It has a very different feel to it than the "I'm going to kick your butt" or "I'm gonna win, you're gonna lose" mentality that we hear more often. It is much more motivating and rewarding to live every moment of the race in your own positive head space, saying, "Yes! I love cornering at this speed, and I'm good at this so I can rise to the challenge." And it's more fun.

Focus on learning skills so that you are confident in your ability to perform them in any situation. Researchers[8] of learning and skill acquisition have observed seven levels of skill competency:

- simply perceiving the skill
- patterning the motion
- adapting to it
- refining it
- varying the skill
- improvising
- and finally composing new variations

[8] National Coaching Certification Program Level I Theory Manual, Coaching Association of Canada, Gloucester, Ontario, Canada.

High-level performers sometimes get to those final two steps. Examples are basketball's Michael Jordan improvising plays during games, hockey's Wayne Gretzky setting up "his office" behind the opponent's net and controlling the play, or high jumper Bill Fosbury composing a new method of clearing the bar, called the "Fosbury Flop."

What skill level are you at now? It can be helpful from time to time to review your skill competency on the following checklist.

Exercise No. 3: Competency inventory

Rate yourself on a scale of zero (I can't) to 10 (excel) on these skills you must be able to do to be successful in your event(s):

Mountain bike: Cross-country
- mass start
- know the course, pick lines—which ones are safe, which save time
- find places to drink, pass, attack, get gaps, close gaps
- riding technical single track
- climbing
- descending
- cornering
- sprinting

Mountain bike: Downhill
Same as cross-country, plus
- starting standing or ramped

- looking further ahead
- high-speed cornering
- braking to control the bike
- pushing the limits of speed
- bike handling

Free riding

Same as downhill, plus

- smoothness
- awareness of other riders
- trials skills

BMX

- acceleration
- using the banking
- flat pedal techniques

Dual slalom

See BMX, plus

- multiple cornering
- sighting lines
- light control on rough terrain
- anticipating

Track pursuit

- standing start
- selecting gearing
- selecting time schedule
- pacing

- aerodynamic equipment
- aerodynamic body position

Team pursuit

Same as in individual pursuit, plus
- sitting closely on a wheel at high speed
- exchange using the banking
- regaining the last wheel
- relaxing while drafting, holding pace, no surging
- execution of final sprint—three to cross the line
- communication with teammates

Points race

- mass start from the railing
- positioning for sprints

POINTS RACERS USE SKILLS FROM SPRINTING AND PURSUITING IN ADDITION TO SKILLS
UNIQUE TO THEIR EVENT.

- gaining a lap (see pursuit skills)
- knowing who else has points
- sprinting
- using the group for lead-outs

Sprints

- sprinting out of the saddle
- gear selection
- accelerating seated sprints
- knowing the opponent's strengths and weaknesses
- watching the opponent
- reaction time
- controlling the opponent
- smoothness and control at maximum leg speed

Kilo

- long, standing start
- selecting gearing
- leg speed
- aerodynamic equipment
- aerodynamic body position

Olympic sprint

See kilo, plus

- team pursuit for starts and exit

Road race, including criterium

- know the course
- pack riding skills—sitting on a wheel, paceline, echelon

and moving up in the pack
- awareness of other riders
- anticipation of attacks
- jump
- gear selection
- reading the wind
- climbing
- sprinting
- using energy wisely
- accelerating
- cornering
- staying close to the front
- descending, judging distances
- communicating with teammates
- eating and drinking
- braking evenly

Touring, centuries and randonneur events
- ride preparation—carrying tools, food, water, lights and map
- route reading
- pacing for long events
- riding in groups
- riding in traffic
- all skills listed under road racing

NOTE: Each of these skills could be further broken down. For example, cornering has steps such as: sighting the best line, adjusting speed, leaning the bike and weighting the outside pedal.

Expand on this inventory with your coach or riding partners. You can also use these inventories as the beginning of a mental script for your event. Talk to your coach or teammates about ways of maximizing skill strengths and minimizing weaknesses.

Physical conditioning and practicing skills are closely linked—you can't do one without affecting the other. Therefore, you can improve both the energy system required for the skill and the skill itself, with the same training.

PEG In training, I usually recommend that you work with a focus on improving weaknesses and maintaining strengths. Racing is different. There, it's smarter to focus on your strengths. Train your weaknesses. Race on your strengths.

Here are a few examples of how to race using your strengths, minimizing your weaknesses:

- A kilo rider can use their long sprinting ability to take a sprint opponent by surprise, initiating the sprint early and going long.
- A sprinter with a great jump will try to hold their opponent behind their wheel until as close to the line as possible, before unleashing their sprint.
- A road rider who is weaker in climbing can go off the front before a long climb, to get a gap that will be slowly closed by the stronger climbers, so the weak climber is still with them at the finish of a climb.
- A good pursuit rider can use their short time trial ability to win prologues, and attack in the final 3 to 4km of a road race to attempt a solo victory.
- A good mountain-bike climber will try to get a large time

gap on the climbing portion of a race, while a good descender does better by staying within range so as to catch up on the downhill instead of trying to keep up on the uphill.

- A strong technical downhiller may take difficult, but faster lines compared to a downhiller who may achieve higher speeds, yet has to brake more often to keep control on the course.

EXERCISE NO. 4: COMPETENCY AFFIRMATIONS

Now that you have an inventory of your strengths and weaknesses, complete these statements to create affirmations of those strengths that you can use in your training and racing.

Competency affirmations

SKILLS:

I am good at _____ (cornering, sprinting, climbing, etc.).

I can anticipate what gear to use when _____.

I love to _____.

Others: _____.

PHYSICAL ATTRIBUTES:

I can hold heart rate ____ bpm for _____ minutes.

I can climb _____ (hill or mountain) in _____ minutes in gear _____.

I sprint all-out in gear _____ for _____ seconds.

I can ride for _____ hours, km or miles.

I can spin gear _____ at cadence _____ rpm, for _____ minutes.

Others: _____

Correcting weaknesses

One way to improve a weakness during training is by matching it with a strength.

PEG A rider who is uncomfortable sitting in a pack but who time trials well, could practice getting comfortable riding with others while performing their time trialing strength in an interval session. In the first interval, the rider can go solo. Then, have another rider accompany them—riding beside them to test their concentration. Next, the rider has to sit on their partner's wheel for short periods of time, gradually increasing the time they sit on the wheel and how close they sit. Continuing the intervals, add another rider on the side. Finally, place riders on both sides so that the rider is surrounded while still sitting on a wheel. Review bike handling drills on the grass prior to these workouts, to warm-up and relax the riders.

To facilitate improvement, it's advisable to introduce the pressure to perform gradually. That means slowing things down at first, especially speed. Perform the task solo, with success, before adding other riders. First, add only one person, then two, then four. You can go through the steps quickly with this pattern. As you experience less anxiety you will build confidence.

Use the following formula for progressing skills:
- solo, slow speed, one task
- solo, faster speed
- pairs, slow speed

PRACTICE SKILLS SOLO BEFORE ADDING SPEED AND OTHER RACERS.

- pairs, faster speed
- two pairs, slower, then faster
- repeat steps with multiple tasks

EXERCISE NO. 5: CORRECTING WEAKNESSES

Here is a method that may help you to correct weaknesses you have identified in Exercise No. 3.

STEP 1

Identify a problem area or skill. For example, fear of descending and cornering on the road makes you back off; fear of mountain-bike race mass starts makes you go out too fast to beat the crowd; your impatience in road races has you attacking too early and later missing the break. If you are unsure of the cause, use your visualization skills to go back into the challenging moment and feel what is going on for you at that time.

A weakness to work on is: _____.

STEP 2

Review the image of a problem moment that you may keep running in your mind, such as a past crash, and listen to the things you are saying to yourself. Stop any negative self-talk like "Here we go again, here's where I get dropped" or "I'm scared, I think I'm going to crash." Replace the scenes with new ones, where you perform the skill better than before, and give yourself encouraging words like "I can do this once." Your example:_____.

STEP 3

Replace the negative self-talk with competency statements, such as, "I corner with confidence." Mentally rehearse the skill. Physically practice the skill some more.

As your skill improves, continue to update your positive statements or self-talk, such as "I can nail this corner, I have done that corner dozens of times." Repeat to instill confidence. Your example: _____.

STEP 4

Continue self-talk with something you love or look forward to. For example, after a climb that is difficult for you, you look forward to the descent. "I can't wait for the descent. The faster I climb, the sooner I get to descend."

Your example: _____.

PEG When making corrections, you will revise your script. Here is a comparison of the old ways that have been corrected with the new sport psych tools:

Old ways:	New:
Visualizes an old crash in a corner.	Visualizes completing a corner successfully.
Says, "I'm scared in corners."	Stops negative talk and says, "I can make the corners."
Avoids the crash corner or slows dramatically.	Practices less intimidating corners solo, at slow speed, then faster, and gradually adds teammates and multiple corners.
Repeats, "I fear/hate cornering."	Says "I can corner well. I can master the corner." Practices cornering, saying, "I love this."

It's a matter of choice. You can choose to continue with your weaknesses, or you can change them with physical and mental practice. The physical element, skill element and mental attitude work together.

Cooperation is another under-used training concept. Training partners have many great benefits. Here are two examples of "using" training partners:

PEG Two riders need to work on their opposite weaknesses. One climbs well by spinning in small gears, the other uses bigger gears in slower cadence. They could train together, side by side, "swapping" strengths. For example, the spinner sits and stands using a bigger gear and slower cadence than normal—more like the teammate, while the normally lower-cadence rider uses lower gears to spin faster than normal. This could be fun, each imitating the other. At 200 meters from the top, the riders could be allowed to revert back to their favorite style to sprint it out, thus including their strengths in the workout as well.

A rider who needs to work on time trialing could be paired with a rider who needs to work on sprinting. The sprinter sits on the time trialer and sprints at designated intervals, then gets back on the steady rider. The time trialer will have the focus of giving a steady lead out for the sprinter, then reeling the sprinter back in. Poor time trialers often lack concentration skills, so this will be a challenge for them to remain focused while the training partner is sprinting.

Opponents can be viewed as helpers and training partners. Remember one of the points made was that we
have a choice. When "stuff" happens, either we "use it" or
"it uses us." Often it is our "sense of deserving" or lack of it
that prevents us from "using the situation."

PEG When the ride gets hard we say to focus on your technique. It's essential to know what skill to focus on, and how
to do it correctly. When you are competent in all the skills
required for your event, when you have trained the energy
system needed for the skill, and when you have positive
thoughts to support the skills, confidence grows.

MENTAL PREPARATION

It is essential that you are gaining confidence about your
mental preparation. Again, writing about your progress in
a journal will support your new mental skill acquisition. Seeing the mental skills in your event script is another concrete
way of documenting your sport psychology repertoire.

As we said earlier, mental preparation consists of emotional control and focus, which we have discussed in chapters one
to four. In chapter five, we began to create scripts of actions
with power thoughts or programs to run during the event.
Now, we bring mental preparation together with your physical
preparation and skill competencies to form a race strategy.

Strategy is the overall race plan. It involves decisions such
as riding conservatively to maintain the race leader's jersey,
riding aggressively to win a one-day event like a national
championship, remaining at the front section of the pack, or
staying below a certain heart rate. Consider your competen-

cies while formulating your strategy, as they represent the core of what you are good at and should be central to your race plan. Consider both your strengths and weaknesses when forming your strategy.

Forming strategy

- Begin by evaluating the course and its demands. A good tactician observes the course first. Remember, "eyes."
- Note the physical demands of a course—hills or windy sections.
- Note technical sections—tight corners or rough surfaces.
- Form a plan.
- Think of the ideal ride.
- Think of what you would like to do in order to excel on the course with your given talents. Consider where to "smooth" and where to "attack."
- Think about who else will be racing and what is at stake for them.
- Think about how that rider may ride the same course.
- Anticipate critical moves a challenger may create during the race.

It is important to think through these moments and to mentally rehearse the options of how and when to respond. During the race, continue to evaluate your status and how other riders are positioning themselves, and note who is alert and who is doing the work in the group.

Adapt your plan to changes in the course or outcome.

For example, the finish line may be in a different place than it was last year, or the fact that there are many categories on the course at once may force you to change your line.

Riders who have done their homework, who have thought about and visualized many different scenarios, will have more options to draw on when revising their strategy, will be more likely to make intelligent choices and will be better able to react quickly.

Every event is unique, and, as such, demands specific strategy and tactics. Each event presents different physical challenges. Each venue has its own characteristics that place additional demands on physical and technical ability. And each rider brings different abilities to the race, so strategy and tactics will be different for each race and for each person.

PEG For example, consider a simple event like track's kilometer. It requires a high degree of lactic-acid tolerance, power and leg speed. It demands the technical ability to have a fast standing start, to pace well and ride smoothly. Velodromes are either 250, 333 or 400 meters in length, so the number of laps it takes to complete 1000 meters varies.

The strength of the wind at the site will help determine what gear the rider will select and when they have to push hard, and where to ease off with the tail wind. In addition, the athlete may be tired, entering additional events, or it may be the nationals or the first track meet of the season. The rider in question may have good leg speed, but lack the ability to hold the effort. All of these components must be considered when forming strategy.

ALAN BOUCHER RUNS THROUGH HIS
SCRIPT PRIOR TO WINNING THE
NATIONAL KILO TITLE.

CHOOSING TO DISMOUNT AND PUSH HIS
BIKE UP THIS SLIPPERY SLOPE IS A
GOOD TACTIC FOR THIS CADET RACER.

EXERCISE NO. 6: SCRIPTING STRATEGY

Once again, describe an upcoming event. This time, script not just yourself racing, but others racing around you, too. Think about "using them" to enhance your performance. Consider the weather, the venue and the time of year. Remember, you deserve to express your ability. To do that, choose to "use" everything.

Reading the race is observing what is going on in the race and adapting your strategy. Observing is the "eyes," seeing who is working hard, who is drinking, where the wind is coming from. Adapting is first questioning if that observation will have any effect on outcome—is a strong rider overdoing it? Will they be tired out later? Are they someone to go with when they attack? Is a competitor dehydrated and out of it? Does the wind's shift mean we will have a tail wind to the finish line? You have to make a judgment on how an observation can affect the outcome. Having good judgment comes from experience and having the emotional control, or patience, to be open to observing the outcomes. Practice questioning and judging by thinking about different scenarios and visualizing how they may play themselves out in the race. When you make a judgment, you still have to react accordingly. There are many options for how to respond to the actions unfolding in the race. Watch races and listen to more experienced riders explain the tactics. In visualizing many different options, you are able to switch tactics more quickly and easily when you recognize the race situation as one of the options you mentally rehearsed.

PEG For example, in preparation for an upcoming race, two riders pre-ride the course. One rider only visualizes the course as they rode it. The other rider visualizes several different lines to take. One line is conservative, dismounting and hiking the bike down a rock face, while another is risky, riding over the rock face. A third line is slower, but avoids the rock face by going around the side. This rider may even go back to that section and physically practice the lines and skills. Come race day, the course is jammed with competitors and spectators. At the rock face the better-prepared rider opts for the slower, wider line to avoid the bottle-neck before the obstacle. The less-prepared rider tries to follow the same line, but has not practiced it physically or mentally, so she tenses and crashes. Meanwhile, the more prepared rider continues around the course and may choose to gain time by going over the rock face the next lap, then safely dismounting at that point in the final lap, to secure her good position.

Debriefing after a race and making notes in your journal can help you to improve the strategy component of cycling competency. Write down a description of the course and the strategy you selected. Describe how the race unfolded and how that changed your plan. Describe the actions you took to adapt. Take note of your preparation routine and your self-talk. Evaluate how they worked for you.

EXERCISE NO. 7: AFFIRMATIONS

Create some affirmations regarding your race- or ride-reading ability by filling in the blanks in these suggested affirmations:

I can plan tactics for the critical parts of _____ race.

I know that the critical move will be made at _____
     part of _____ race.

I am ready to be aggressive at _____ part of the race
     and ready to conserve and observe during the _____
     section.

Others: _____.

Inferences:

Since I can _____, therefore, I can _____.

(Example: "Since I can sprint all out in 53 x 15 for 44 seconds, I can jump first, 400 meters to go, in the final sprint"; "Because I can climb rough, rocky terrain in the middle ring,

I can do Sunday's cross-country race in the middle ring for the uphill start"; "Because I can spin the 50 x 15 at 110 rpm, I can do a 3000-meter pursuit in that gear.)

Maintain a positive attitude to support your strategy. There are several aspects to an optimal cycling attitude. In chapter five we discussed the basics: commitment, confidence, identity and deserving. To reiterate, a winning attitude begins with motivation. That involves defining clear goals and the commitment to make them happen. As we said before, commitment is being willing to do the work necessary to realize your goals.

We have said, "see it, believe it, do it."

There are several aspects of belief that relate to competency.

Confidence is a sense of faith that you can endure and excel. Confidence is nurtured through preparation and success. You can develop confidence by defining the elements that you need to excel in your event. Then, do the necessary physical, skill and mental training to perform these elements well. Finally, develop a race strategy that incorporates your training and maximizes your ability.

Identity is that sense of who you are that grows with time and experience of facing life's challenges in that forum called cycling. It's saying to yourself, "I am somebody who can do that." A positive identity is something that can empower you and lift your performance.

Deserving is a sense or belief that frees you to express your ability. Just as you deserve your time to breathe. You deserve to express all of your ability. These four elements of attitude are interactive. Similarly, the elements of competency interact and interrelate. Physical training, skill training and mental training grow confidence. Confidence and a sense of deserving liberate you to express your power and skill.

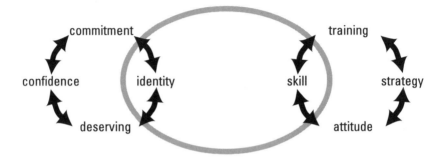

Flashback: At the highest levels, competency represents several elements.

- It's about having done the physical work, the miles and hours, aerobic and anaerobic training, the strengths and cross-training. It's about understanding how to operate your mental television, and being able to change channels and maintain emotional control. It's about having a productive focus, running positive programs, power words and high-performance images. It's about being clear, tuning out distractions and negativity, and maintaining a positive, productive attitude.
- Another major part of competency is having the technique and skill to handle the bicycle in a variety of ride and race circumstances, such as cornering with speed, racing across difficult terrain, descending with speed, climbing, sprinting, riding in crowds and riding under pressure.
- A third aspect of competency relates to using your mental skills to make good decisions about how to ride the

race. This involves having a pre-race strategy, a blueprint of how to ride the race that enhances anticipation and sets you up to excel. What's equally important is having the ability to read the race as it unfolds, and adapting your strategy for maximum efficiency and impact.

Races like a kilo, mountain-bike downhill or time trial may be fully scripted.

For other events, like a mountain-bike cross-country, road race or points race, strategy is more complex, and it's essential to be able to read the situation, be flexible and adapt. And finally, it's about being mentally tough and maintaining a positive, productive attitude.

How would you evaluate competency?

There are three major elements that go into being a competent bicycle racer. They are being:

- physically fit and having done the physical training
- skilled and having the skill sets to climb, corner, descend and sprint
- mentally prepared, which has a number of elements including: emotional control (chapters one and two); focus (chapter three and four); and having a script and mentally rehearsing (chapter five)
- a strategy or plan
- being able to read a race or ride and adapt your strategy to your situation
- maintaining a positive, productive, high-performance focus and attitude

PEG I have observed that athletes train a lot. They train for physical preparation, and because they enjoy doing their sport. Because cycling is such a physically demanding sport, it's not surprising that cyclists do so much physical training to prepare for their events. There are awareness benefits that come from the physical training. Each time you sit in the saddle it's an opportunity to learn about your response to the physical demands cycling presents. Listen to what you say to yourself when you are in the saddle.

During a cyclo-cross race in California, I caught myself saying, "You're no good at this. Why are you even out here?" Those are such harsh words for an athlete who placed fourth in the national championships in that event. I suppose I was feeling tired, sloppy, not up to the challenge of dismounting and carrying my bike over the giant Redwood trunk and up and over the picnic table. What if I were to support and encourage myself, instead? When I heard myself saying those destructive words, I changed my thoughts and breathed deeply. Then I told myself, "I love cyclo-cross." It is very hard work, harder than any criterium I have raced as I carry my bike on dead legs, instead of it carrying me. I would say, "I love having to time my dismounts," and then automatically place my right hand through the frame to lift it onto my shoulder, my feet trotting under me. My front wheel slipped in the mud on a downhill left turn and I heard my breathing rasp in my throat on a grassy uphill, but I said, "I am good at this and I enjoy all these sensations." It's easier to say the negative because 85 percent of what we hear each day is negative. That's why it is important to plan what we say to ourselves when we are writing our cycling scripts. Plan for success, say encouraging words to yourself.

Each time you go out on your bike you learn about yourself. You are response-able to acquire the kind of self-knowledge about your cycling that gives you confidence. Know that your physical training is contributing to your preparation. Know you can perform the skills necessary for the event. Know that you are mentally prepared for any situation. Combine this awareness. Repeat these positive thoughts. Cultivate confidence by affirming that you are a competent racer.

HOMEWORK

1. Think of an example of when you mastered a skill. Remember the positive thoughts you had, and what you said to yourself. Recreate the positive image or mastering that element and mentally rehearse it. Now, take that same mindset to a different skill—one you've struggled with—and visualize it. Note any differences in your mindset from how you have imagined that skill in the past?

2. Use the competency checklist and affirmations (Exercises Nos. 3 and 4) to create six new power thoughts.

3. Think of an example of when you have been mentally tough, when you have not given up at a skill or game. Compare that to a time when you gave up or quit. What is the difference in your mental states? Find positive statements that can help you, then visualize redoing the second example with more confidence.

4. The script you have been creating should include power thoughts, self-talk, affirmations, imagery, attitude, identity, skills—don't forget skills—and your awareness of other competitors. Now, add to the script: strategy, tactics, mental toughness and focus terms you reviewed in this chapter. This will complete your script. Remember, it is called a script because, like a movie script, it has action, sound and emotional content.

HOMEWORK REVIEW

COMMENTS FROM PEG

1. The cyclists in our workshop had trouble recalling exactly what they were thinking and what they did when they performed a skill with mastery. That's because it came so easily to them, it was hard to remember each step. Athletes who teach their sport skills to others have usually gone through this process. They know how to break down the skill for novice cyclists. Often, they recall how confident they felt, how they mentally reviewed the steps of the skill before executing the skill. They were relaxed, focused and enjoyed the moment.

2. The cyclists seemed to have more confidence in their power thoughts when they came up with them based on their own competency. We heard statements such as:

"I can climb in whatever gear I choose. I can dance on the pedals."

"I love to corner with speed. I can lead the pack into the last corner, and come through the turn first and fastest to win the race."

"I can time trial faster and faster. My rolling resistance forms an electrical charge that surrounds and energizes me. I shift to a harder gear and pedal faster."

3. Again, riders were reluctant to give themselves credit for times they "hung tough." Riders helped each other to remember races in the rain, riding with broken spokes, continuing after a flat tire. Riders had lots of examples of others who were tough in order to finish the race.

4. Here is a script example from a downhiller. First he reviewed the script he actually ran at the nationals, then we corrected it to make it more effective:

Script 1

"Before my run at Silver Star, I was very nervous as to be expected—it's the nationals, but at the same time I was relaxed having spent many days on the course. I knew that all I needed was a clean run, and I would place well. The course was dry, rocky and constantly changing, so a lot of guys would be making mistakes. The course was also short, and favored a technical BMX style. It's because of these things that I was feeling confident as I rolled up to the start ramp. This is always a good time to focus on the top of the course. The first section is a flat sprint across the Alberta Flats into some sketchy corners and then another flat sprint.

"Riding the top section smoothly was important to my confidence for the entire race. This is mostly because a clean start lets me clear my head for what's to come. Sometimes a bobble or mistake will cast a cloud over my confidence, so the start is crucial. Off the top sprint, I dropped into the Air BC drop and hammered the rough uphill, squeaked around a flat corner, and cruised into the first nasty section. As in practice, I hit my line, then railed the switchback corners. The whole time in the corners I had Pintos Pitch chewing at the back of my brain. This is a really rough, fall-away rock face that gave a lot of people problems. I hit the pitch and made a big mistake, that would eventually cost me the race. I didn't fall, but it really wouldn't matter, in my mind I lost time, but not nearly as much as I could have saved by staying focused.

"After the mistake in Pintos Pitch, I altered my game plan and turned it up a notch. I pedaled harder into the approach for the Hound Dog drop than ever before and jumped a gap I only thought about in practice. This is right where the old and the new race courses come together, so the next corner I had ridden a hundred times—without crashing. Well, I crashed. Now, whether this is because of overconfidence, or the extra speed from the Hound drop, I don't know. Probably a combination of both, but regardless this is where the crash in Pintos Pitch cost me the race. By letting my mistake change my race, I inevitably lost it.

"Now comes the toughest mental battle of any race, trying to salvage a lost run. Hammering down the bottom half all I could think of was my national ranking. This distraction would explain my scary crash into the high speed Barf Up section. Another section where I had never fallen, thus proving how lapses in my mental game blew my nationals hopes. My only hope now was to save face by blasting the bottom section, flying into the finish.

"I crossed the line exhausted, frustrated and disappointed in myself. This is where the mental battle continues, and will keep on until next season. It would be easy to let the situation get me down, but there is really no point. It feels a lot better to be satisfied with the fact that I tried my best, and have a good time at the party. I'll get them next year!"

Script 2

What follows is a revised version of the same script that has been edited to be more effective:

"Before my run at Silver Star, I breathe deeply and relax my shoulders. I review the course in my mind. Knowing that I have practiced it physically and mentally gives me confidence. I know the way to do well on this course is to have a clean run that also pushes my limits. The course is currently dry and rocky, but is changing constantly. I can handle a variety of terrain conditions and can choose the lines and skills they require and that allows me to continue to make good choices.

"Riding the top section smoothly and cleanly is my goal. I want to set the tone for my run. If I make a mistake or bobble, I will not let it affect the next section. I change the channel and focus on the upcoming demands. Off the top sprint I take the Air BC drop. I hammer the rough-up hill and whip around the flat corner. I look forward to the first nasty section.

"I hit my line and this sets me up to rail the switchback corners. Pintos Pitch is coming up, but I switch my thinking to the task at hand, speeding down the trail. I exhale and release tense muscles before the fall-away rock face and let my body absorb the impact as I have done many times in practice. I am in auto-control mode, and time is slowing down.

"I am through Pintos Pitch. Wow, I cleaned it! Approaching the Hound Dog drop I have plenty of speed and I leap into the air—I have mentally rehearsed this and I push my limits, never having done this jump before in practice. My solid landing is an awesome reward. I slow my breathing to control my excitement, my pounding heart. I get centered again and refocus. What's next? I'm reaching the end of the old course and I hit the high-speed corner, loving the sliding fast sound. Smoothing the remainder of this section allows me to regroup before the bottom part of the course.

"Now I up my effort, cranking on the pedals. I calculate my speed and adjust before going into the Barf Up section. I smooth the rough spots and have a few turns to go. I lean into the lines, straighten up and sprint all the way past the finish line. I have succeeded; I have done my best."

SPOT CHECK: SIGNS OF OVERTRAINING

We all know how easy it is to see the mistakes made by other riders. For example, we can see how Joe is overtraining, or we notice how poorly Fred corners and makes more work for himself by creating gaps. It's often more difficult to see and accept if you are overtrained, unless you step back and take a careful look at yourself.

Pretend you are looking at yourself as if you are another rider.

Here are some classic signs of overtraining. Can you see these signs in this rider?

- Fatigue
- Experiencing sleep extremes: either sleeplessness or needing extra sleep

- Clumsiness
- Irritability, moodiness
- High resting heart rate, which is your pulse taken usually in the mornng before getting up, measured in beats per minute
- Difficulty getting heart rate up in training, combined with slower than normal speeds for a given effort level
- Recurrent infections—frequent colds, canker sores, blisters, saddle sores—that don't seem to heal
- Loss of appetite
- Loss of desire to ride

Keeping an objective training diary will also help to point out these symptoms. More rest or lighter training is often the prescription for any of these signs of overtraining, but if you are uncertain, or if symptoms persist, it's important to consult a good sports medical physician.

While counseling a teenage athlete, I asked her what things limited her. She replied, "fatigue." "Well," I said, "fatigue can be a sign that you are tired and that you need more rest, or it may mean you are facing an obstacle that you want to avoid. You are usually the best person to judge what fatigue really means for you, and to make the right decision as to what to do."

It is very important to determine the etiology of a cyclist's lack of energy. Is their "apparent overtraining" more attributable to a physical or mental cause? It would make matters worse to continue to push through when rest is needed. In your quest to be an optimal cyclist, be aware of balancing the pursuit and push to excellence with being sensitive and kind to yourself. Read the signs, grow your judgment and in the face of uncertainty consult with an experienced coach and sport medical physician.

CHAPTER SEVEN

Individual
differences

"Socrates said, 'Know yourself.' It's a good idea, since everyone is unique. The performance trick is to find ways to use your strengths and develop your weaknesses. Ride your strengths hard and celebrate your uniqueness quietly."
—Dr. Miller

"It doesn't matter who you beat or what you win, it's over when you cross the line. To be happy with your performance you have to compare yourself to yourself."
—Peg

The goal of chapter seven is to describe some of the differences that exist among cyclists in regard to personality style, and to suggest ways that you can adapt your training and racing strategy to maximize performance and satisfaction.

In chapter five we discussed several qualities of a winning attitude. I would like to add another quality to the list. It's what I call a sense of deserving.

None of the qualities that we spoke about is completely separate from the others.

Deserving relates to qualities of confidence and identity.

confidence

deserving   identity

Confronted with a sprint or breakaway situation, some

cyclists "jump." They just go for it. It's as if they feel that they deserve the opportunity, and they're going to take it. Other cyclists don't feel as confident or deserving, and they give it up or let it go. It's the same with mountain biking and time trialing, where some riders just seem to think, "I deserve it. It's mine. I'm going for it. I am. I can." It's believing that you deserve to express all of your ability to excel. "The opportunity is there and I am going to fill it with my ability." "Even if it's not there, I'll take it anyway." There's no evident doubt, inhibition or holding back.

It frequently happens in competitive situations that a cyclist looks over the field and sees other riders they perceive to be more experienced than themselves. It is often someone who has beaten them in the past or someone who has won at higher levels. At times like that the cyclist's energy may drop and a part of them thinks, "I'm not that good." And with that thought may come the feeling, "I don't deserve it as much as they do." Then, as thinking affects performance, they go out and prove themselves right by riding an inferior race. If you don't believe you deserve it, it's unlikely you're going to make it happen.

What I have found to be useful in helping athletes who don't feel deserving or confident about their ability in a particular situation is to have them go back to a feeling state where they do feel empowered, and build from there.

Indeed, if ever you create feelings of "not deserving," then, take a momentary "time out," generate a good feeling state, empower yourself and affirm, "I deserve to feel good and I deserve to express my ability."

EXERCISE NO. 1: DESERVING

Sit back and get into your breathing.

First, as always, tune into your breathing rhythm.

As you do, remind yourself that you deserve this time.

Experience that you deserve the time it takes for the breath to come in, and go out.

This is not just about understanding a concept, but rather experiencing a feeling.

As you begin to experience your breathing you'll know, truthfully, that you deserve this time.

Next, imagine riding your bicycle. Imagine riding well, with ease and good form, and with speed and power. As you do, affirm that you deserve to express your ability, all of your ability. Again, know and actually feel that you deserve to express your ability.

Now, bring that awareness and sense of deserving to the moment, to the race or ride at hand. If you find yourself in a race with more experienced riders, and with people who have beat you in the past, and if you start to feel less than powerful and less deserving than them, use their presence to remind you to go deeper into the breathing; inspire and empower yourself; experience those good feelings and acknowledge what you know to be true. "I deserve my time." "I deserve to express my ability." Then, bring that sense of deserving into the race.

Some athletes are uncertain about how much they deserve to be competitive. Ann was a sprint cyclist who had entered the competitive track racing scene relatively late. She was powerful and fast, but at times her lack of experience undermined her confidence. Furthermore, she presented herself as a very considerate, well-mannered person. She was someone who certainly wouldn't take something that didn't belong to her. Indeed, her sense of deserving was moderated by a large dose of inhibition. As a world-class competitor, her apparent lack of deserving sometimes allowed her opponent to take the race.

I consulted with her prior to the medal round of an important international competition. In the sprint semi-finals she had excellent position coming around the final turn, but didn't seem to believe she could do it. She didn't make her move, and her opponent did and won. Now she was competing for the bronze medal against another experienced rider—someone not as strong and fast as her. I sensed her nervousness and uncertainty. I encouraged her to breathe. As she began to feel more calm I reminded her that she deserved to express her ability—all of it.

"It's just you in this race," I said. "Just you against you. The other rider is simply here to push you to be at your best. The question is, how good can you be?" Seeing the race as a personal challenge, and having been given the okay to be aggressive, express all of her ability, and go for it, she did. And she won the next two heats and the medal.

As we said in chapter five, avoid focusing on other riders or comparing yourself to them. It is a way of giving away your power. Instead, see the race as a personal exercise, an opportunity for you to be your best. If in a moment of doubt you start comparing yourself to others, use that awareness to go back to turning the wheel and reminding yourself, "I deserve to express my ability. They are just here to give me an opportunity to excel."

If you get intimidated by the competition, change your focus. Instead of going out there to destroy them, frame it that you are out there to excel, to enjoy and to shine. You deserve to express it all. That's what optimal performance is about.

Your feelings and confidence are completely within your area of control. It's been said many times that a person can't always control their circumstances. However, you can control your reactions to them. You control the sense of deserving to be your best.

PEG It took me more than one season to stop always playing domestique, automatically blocking for teammates in breaks when I was right there when the break formed and I could have been in it, too. Things began to change when I began to say to myself over and over, "I deserve to be in the break." I visualized being right in there when breaks formed, and pulling through. Then gradually it began to happen: I began to feel more confident, and when I recognized a break forming, I pulled through instead of backing off. My race results improved dramatically.

Once I retired from international racing, I would easily win local races. I just knew what moves to make, where to position myself, and when to go. I deserved it and I just went for it. I continued to win against national team riders simply by thinking that I had already earned the win based on my experience and who I was as a racer.

INDIVIDUAL DIFFERENCES

In the first six chapters we have outlined the basic mental training principles and skills for optimal cycling. These principles and techniques are applicable to everyone.

Of course, people are different. In this chapter we are going to discuss individual differences, both in terms of how people differ from each other, and how different cycling events make different demands on a rider.

Let's talk first about how people differ from each other and how these differences may affect how you prepare, how you deal with pressure, and how you ride and race.

There are many ways to differentiate between people. One psychological test that I frequently use is the Myers Briggs Type Indicator. It looks at personality style on four separate dimensions. The three that are most relevant to our discussion are called: extroversion versus introversion, knowledge versus intuition, and feeling versus thinking.

They represent three ways of looking at the many differences between people.

You may recall in chapter two we said that there is a direct

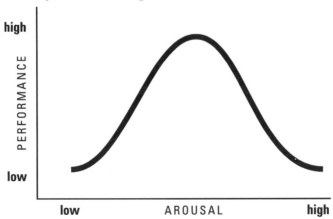

relationship between performance and the amount of stimulation or emotional arousal a person experiences. With either
too much or too little arousal, performance is less than optimal. The relationship is depicted in the graph (facing page).

Extroversion-introversion

The relationship is complicated with the introduction of
individual differences and personality style variables such as
introversion and extroversion. In general, introverts tend to be
more sensitive and overload more easily than extroverts.
Extroverts are more stimulus-seeking and require more arousal
to be at their best. That relationship is depicted as follows.

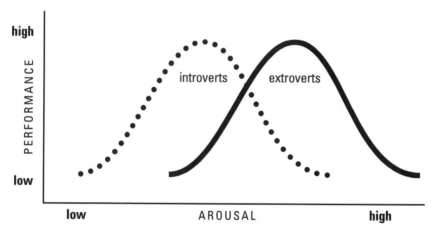

What this means in terms of ride preparation and race
behavior is that introverts tend to avoid excessive stimulation, including surprise, immediately prior to competition. In
contrast, extroverts tend to be more stimulus-seeking and
may actually require stimulation and interaction to get into
their optimal arousal zone.

INTROVERTS

To reduce stimulation, introverts prefer things to be structured. They like to know what's going on. To avoid chaos and any unnecessary surprises, they seem to function better with a clearly defined schedule and routine. They prefer to create a pre-ride schedule and stick to it. Disorder is arousing and disturbing, so they avoid rushing and they take precautions to prevent any last-minute surprises. They like things to be on time. They will take the time to see that their equipment is in order. This is a useful quality. However, sometimes introverts obsess or become preoccupied with the details and ritual of preparation. To allay any potential anxiety it can be useful to remind them, or yourself, to relax; reassure them that everything will be fine and on time.

EXTROVERTS

Likewise, extroverts may experience difficulty in organizing well in advance. They tend to wait until the urgency of the last minute to get them going. This can lead to confusion. Extroverts are more inclined to be disorganized about equipment and scheduling. They are more inclined to leave things unattended until the last minute. It is advisable to remind them to schedule time to address ride and race preparation.

It is important to be aware of who you are, and who your teammates are, and to respect the differences that exist between people. You deserve to express your abilities, and so do they.

PEG We were so different on our team of five. Before a race, some of us liked to listen to loud rock, some liked heavy metal, some liked classical music, and some wanted to be quiet. Discussing this in a team meeting, we decided that on race day we could each have what we wanted, and what matched our personality style, by listening to our own Walkmans instead of playing anything on the van's stereo. It certainly worked for introverted me, and it seemed to work for everyone.

Another thing we agreed upon was to warm down after a race before talking about it. It helped those of us who needed to calm down after an exciting finish, so in our haste and excitement we wouldn't say anything we'd regret later. It was also a wise move not to show any outbursts to the post-race media. It helped us to get perspective before rehashing how it went. We also agreed to keep any team problems within the team and team meetings, so we could trust each other and show unity before our competitors. We all understood that and valued the effect.

EXERCISE NO. 2: INDIVIDUALIZING YOUR STRATEGY

We have enclosed pre-competition and competition strategy sheets that provide a way of scheduling your time and energy from the day before the race, right up to and through the race. This is useful because it will give you a clear mental picture of what you will be experiencing, which will enable you to plan, prepare and visualize effectively. All of which will build confidence.

Complete the strategy sheets in Appendix C for an upcoming competition.

Introverts are more inclined to fill in inventories and keep a journal.

Extroverts may require more reminders and supervision to be organized and on time.

Not attending to these differences is something that can cause rider or team problems, even (especially) at the highest levels of competition.

Another distinction between introverts and extroverts is that extroverts prefer people around them before a race. They often enjoy being interactive, social, joking with friends and competitors, even challenging them. Introverts, on the other hand, are more apt to prepare quietly and alone, often mentally rehearsing the race with imagery or warming up quietly on their own. Socializing can be a disturbing distraction for them.

Again, understanding who you are and what style works for you can be very helpful. One thing you can do to gain insight is to recall those days when you rode at your best. Think back, and ask yourself, "What did I do to prepare on those high-performance days?"

EXERCISE No. 3: BEST PERFORMANCE

Go back and visualize an event where you performed to the best of your ability. Fill out the forms based on your activities that day. Then do the same for a not-so-rewarding event. Compare the two so that the differences will stand out and you will be able to clearly identify the pre-race routine that works for you.

An athlete came up to me after a talk I gave on performance at a conference. He was an introverted, task-oriented and hyper-analytical young man. He told me that he had recently experienced the unfortunate family incident of the death of his father. A day or two later he was asked to compete in a major competition. He couldn't decide what to do. Late at night before the event he said to himself, "I'm going to compete and I'm going to do it for my dad." He competed and won. In retrospect, he thought that he won because he dedicated the event to his dad, and because his last-minute decision to compete didn't allow him the time to ruminate about all the details that he normally becomes obsessed with prior to competi-

SOME RIDERS LIKE TO WARM UP ALONE. FIND OUT WHAT WORKS BEST FOR YOU.

tion. He said he now appreciates the extent to which his excessive inner focus affected his performance in the past. Understand who you are and give yourself a little flexibility around that preferred pattern you have.

Feeling-thinking

Another personality style difference between people is that some are more task-oriented, while others are more people-oriented. What is relevant, is the relative extent to which you focus on the task you are preparing for—as compared to a social interest and awareness you may have around the event. It is also about the perspective you have and how you prefer to be acknowledged.

PEG As I became more adaptable and more people-oriented, I began to feed off my teammates and enjoyed racing even more. For example, my teammate Sue said, "This should be a good race for you," prior to a short time trial. I was thinking that it would be a good course for her and shared that with her. In the past, I would have preferred to warm up solo and would have missed receiving that encouragement from her. The camaraderie that is built over simple exchanges like that can be very strong. I once dropped out of a race to help her when she crashed. I remember supporting her while she leaned against me as we waited for help, her face bloodied and her body shaking.

Feeling-oriented people are more social. They are concerned with feelings: how they feel, how others feel, and of course, how others see and feel about them in return. They tend to respond to a pat on the back. They appreciate people acknowledging them for who they are. They seek out comments such as, "You are a good rider" and "You are someone I can really count on." They are often upset by others saying negative or uncomplimentary things about them.

Task-oriented people are primarily focused and concerned with the elements of the task at hand, with breaking it down, analyzing what has to be done and doing it. They are less sensitive to acknowledgment and are most responsive to being acknowledged for their competency. At times, they may seem less sensitive to the needs of other cyclists on the team or to supportive people because their focus is on the task. It is useful for all team members to be aware that there are individual differences and that some cyclists focus much more on the task and their equipment, while others are more socially interested and involved.

What's important is to understand who you are and to have the flexibility and balance to express your style in preparation and training.

Knowledge-intuition

Another personality dimension that differentiates people is that some folks are more analytical and detail-oriented ("S" on the Meyers Briggs Type Indicator), while others are generalizers ("N"). The S people are more detailed and specific. They sharpen and highlight differences. They can be exacting, and focus on small imperfections. They enjoy creating and maintaining order. As part of their preparation they often break the race course down into small components, incorporating these into their mental rehearsal. They may consider in detail how they will perform on each section. Sometimes, they have to be encouraged to step back and take a look at "the big picture" or the predominant pattern—for example, the line of the course—as opposed to focusing on each detail or rock on the trail.

The generalizers—N people—see the big picture. They can sense the line and the flow. However, they must be reminded of the detail and specifics—the rocks and roots in certain places—to anticipate and avoid. While the N generalizers tend to pass over or skip detail, the S sharpeners are more apt to focus on detail and sometimes be slowed by it. If you are coaching an N generalizer remember that he or she may benefit from encouragement to bring a little more detailed focus to their perspective.

As we have said throughout, a good suggestion is to go back to those days when you really excelled and reflect on your preparation for that race or ride.

If you go through the precompetition and competition strategy sheets, you will see that they encompass everything you will need to do to prepare including:

- what time to get up
- what to visualize
- what to eat
- the activities you do
- when to rest
- how to go about checking your equipment
- when to check it
- when to leave for the course
- checking equipment again before the race
- what to mentally rehearse
- reviewing race strategy
- what warm-up routine you want to experience
- what timelines you want to have
- what you are saying to yourself
- how to relax if you are feeling tense
- key words to have for yourself
- your immediate pre-race and race focus

Again, the people who are more introverted, and more task- and detail-oriented are more likely to approach this evaluation with more interest, ease and enthusiasm, and their report is apt to be more thorough. It's less difficult to encourage introverts to do this. While it can be useful to get those who are more extroverted to record observations, it may be a challenge to get them to do it.

JOURNALING

Journaling is an ongoing process of maintaining these kind of pre-ride and competition observations. It involves making notes on your goals, plans, experience of the training process, the actual ride and any significant post-race observations. It can be a useful personal record. It involves distilling your observations, and providing yourself with guidelines and feedback on how you are doing. It's important to be clear as to why you are keeping a performance record. Some people who are very focused on detail may have copious notes including some excellent observations, but lose sight of why and what they are gleaning from journal writing. In contrast, others are very casual about journal writing and end up with sketchy, generalized commentary that is so vague and indifferent that it will not be particularly useful.

Journaling is an important part of watching and observing your cycling process. It is something that can provide you with clear feedback of your various competitions or challenges. With good journal notes you can always go back to answer that question, "What did I do (or not do) on that day l really excelled?" You have a personal record of it. It is a kind of debriefing process.

PEG Throughout my racing career, I always found journal writing to be a very helpful training aid. The following are excerpts from my journal when I was racing.

MARCH 8 CAMP MAYBRY POINTS RACE CRITERIUM

Concentrated on positioning, so pleased. Came 11th—need to put in that extra effort at the end. Think I need to use smaller gears and spin more so I don't tire as easily.

(In this short note, there is an acknowledgment of something well done—positioning well, concentrating—plus analysis and tasks to work on in upcoming races.)

MARCH 10 LEON SPRINGS ROAD RACE

Felt lousy at first. Using smaller gears helped. I bridged after one-and-one-fifth laps to the break, felt great. Smart sprint off Betsy King's wheel. First!!!

(This entry reminds me that I can start off feeling poorly, but make the right tactical moves and end up winning a race. I also felt better later and can remind myself that when I don't feel well at the beginning of a race it might change. Again, there is a comment of praise for correcting previous error of over-gearing.)

MARCH 17 COWTOWN CRITERIUM

Six corners, deadly cobblestones. Always up front. Won one prime. Good work opening gaps to help teammates form breaks. Led out sprint. Left the corner open and Jeannie Longo took advantage, jumping through for the win. I could have won if I had been more aware of the gap behind us—I didn't have a teammate on my wheel after all. Second.

(This race analysis reminds me how important it is to ride at the front, especially where the course is tight. I liked how I took responsibility for my actions of not being aware of who was or wasn't on my wheel, rather than blaming my teammates for not being there.)

There are additional journal writing examples in Appendix A.

External-internal

Some people are very externally oriented. They focus more on the things around them and pay less attention to how they feel and what is going on inside them. Externally oriented people have the ability to read a race situation and sense what's going on with the field—who's doing what, and what's where. However, they may not read their own state well and may pace poorly—over-extending by doing too much early in a race, chasing down too many breaks and then fading at the end.

The flip side of the coin is represented by those people who are very internally oriented. While they may have a clear idea of how they feel, they may be considerably less cognizant of what is going on around them. There is a tendency for very internally oriented people to become hyper-reflective and excessively focused on their anxieties.

PEG Athletes that are too internally oriented may be strong, but they can miss the critical moves in the race like attacking on a single-track downhill or a long climb.

They may spend so much time thinking about how they are feeling and assessing themselves that they don't see a breakaway form off the front or they get boxed in during a sprint. To read the race better and be more successful they need to shift some of their focus to the course or the other riders.

One way an internally focused rider can increase their external focus is to use the strategy sheets to preview and determine what is important in the race course—the wind's direction, or whether it is faster to run with your bike in a technical section or to ride it out—and then script themselves on the course. Breaking the course down into sections can broaden the focus by showing the rider how many options they have within the race. It's a good idea to evaluate the course and plan how to respond to the moves the other riders make. Another way to increase external focus is with observation drills. For example, in a criterium the rider reports what position they were in for each lap of the race.

In chapter two we spoke about eyes. The optimal cyclist uses his or her eyes to sense internal and external stimuli.

Visualization differences

Visualization is another area where individual differences come into play. There are differences in the way people visualize themselves cycling both in regard to perspective and sensory qualities. With mental rehearsal, most cyclists report that they imagine themselves riding a race from the perspective of seeing the race through the eyes of someone on the bicycle. It's as if they are in the saddle going over the hill and around the corner and through the straightaway.

Other cyclists report having a kind of bird's eye view, or video style. For them it's as though they are sitting back somewhat removed, watching themselves ride their bike from afar. It's as if they are up in the stands. Both styles seem to work. I am inclined to encourage cyclists to use the former.

PEG I use the bird's eye view for rehearsing technical sections or intense efforts such as the pursuit. I use the video style to "fast-forward" through long events like cross-country or road races.

Imagery really is a multisensory experience. Imagining yourself on a bicycle can also stimulate kinesthetic

WALTER LAI DESIGNS

SOME CYCLISTS VISUALIZE WHAT THEY SEE FROM THEIR OWN EYES.

ROBERT MAJOR

OTHERS VISUALIZE THEMSELVES AS IF SOMEONE WERE VIDEOTAPING THEM.

and tactile elements that will enrich your mental training. The kinesthetic component includes images like powering the pedals, pulling on the handlebars, the feeling of sending energy out the top of the head as in "knifing," experiencing the sense of speed in descent, and the feeling of the wind and speed as you hammer.

Tactile and kinesthetic feelings are more easily and powerfully experienced when you use your "on the bike eyes" in imagery. Experiment with both kinds of imagery. Use what works best for you.

What we're saying is that people choose to respond to pressure in different ways. Know yourself. Evaluate your patterns and style. Grow your awareness. Remember the wisdom of balance. And make good choices.

The bottom line is whether what you choose to do <u>enhances your ability to perform, especially under pressure.</u>

Some riders make a very quick study of the courses they are going to ride. For others, analyzing the ride is a much more lengthy, detailed process.

PEG Alison Sydor says she has gotten very good at memorizing courses quickly because riders often don't get access to a World Cup course for more than one test ride.

In contrast, 1990 world downhill champion Cindy Devine pre-rode the world's downhill course 14 times before her gold medal run. That is actually a conservative amount, as she used visualization to get in dozens more runs, which saved wear and tear on her body, equipment and the course. Visualization is increasingly the practice of choice for top racers.

Cindy was also the first to warm up using a magnetic resistance trainer at the top of the course. After observing her preparation at a World Cup, I said I couldn't see how she was getting enough warm-up just spinning around at the rocky summit. She took a lot of flack from friends as we lugged the equipment up to the top. She hid out of sight, but warmed up on the trainer, closing her eyes to visualize the course, then "riding" it on the trainer, standing when she would stand during the race, leaning, braking, as if she were actually descending. She took home another bronze medal that year in Bromont, Québec. The next year in France, we had to fight for room at the top to place the trainer. The Italians were all warming up on them, too.

Returning to our comparison of personality styles: extroverts are more stimulus-seeking than introverts. Their imagery tends to be shorter and at the last minute. Introverts prefer a schedule and a more quiet precompetition routine. Immediately before competition, the introvert may be more inclined to use relaxation, while the extrovert may be just as likely to "pump-up" and use that energy surge to help them prepare to excel.

Many cyclists monitor their competition-feeling state-of-mind by measuring heart rate (see "Spot Check," chapter five). Some, usually introverts, measure heart rate or count their pulses before a race to see if they have a certain predetermined pulse rate, which means that they are in an optimal zone. If not, they will either calm themselves down or pump themselves up with breathing, self-talk and music. It's a matter of learning what feels "right" and what works—and doing it.

Take a careful look at who you are. As you complete the precompetition and competition strategy sheets, reflect on those days when you really excelled. What seemed to work for you?

Determine what your preferred training and pre-race patterns are.

If you are not clear, then it may be time to make some

Coaching

Coaching others provides an excellent opportunity and challenge to understand the marked range of individual differences that exist between people. The same individual differences that play among athletes can be found among coaches. Coaches can be introverted or extroverted, feeling- or task-oriented, detail people or generalizers—and with maturity and experience have a practical awareness of both.

A coach's personality style can interact with a rider's personality. For example, an introverted coach may readily understand the needs of an introverted cyclist and allow him or her more time and space to prepare. The introvert-ed coach is more apt than his extroverted counterpart to sense the introverted rider's sensitivity, and to support a training and competition structure that reduces stress.

Of course, an introverted coach has some of the same needs as an introverted athlete. In addition to teaching strategy and technique, the introverted coach is challenged to display the necessary flexibility, understanding and communication skills in dealing with a more outgoing, spontaneous, extroverted athlete.

Similarly, an extroverted coach who can appreciate an extrovert's appetite for input, and even confrontation, would find it easier to respond to this careful observations.

Cycling challenges can provide an opportunity to learn more about who you are, and what you can do in order to enhance your response-ability.

Change and experience

Another aspect of individual differences to consider relates to the concept of change. Just as a child grows and behavior. At the same time, the coach must impose the necessary order and structure on the extroverted athlete. Similarly, an extroverted coach must adjust his or her style to the more sensitive style of the introverted athlete.

The same things can be said about the very task-oriented coach having more clarity and understanding in communicating with task-oriented athletes, and being challenged to support the more feeling-minded cyclist. Or, the coach who is more detail-oriented may work more easily with similar styled athletes and may have to make an effort to help generalizers appreciate the value of detail in their preparation. Indeed, whenever there is a personality style difference between cyclist and coach, both parties should remember to breathe in order to exercise a little more patience and flexibility.

The ideal coaching situation, whether you are a coach or an athlete, is to get in touch with who you are and learn how to put yourself into your optimal zone, and then how to relate from there. Clearly, there are different ways to do this for people with differing personality styles. And there are different ways to coach athletes to help them to perform at their best.

Remember, whether you are an extrovert or an introvert, a coach or a racer, everyone can benefit from remembering to take a couple of breaths, spin the wheel and focus on a power word or a high-performance image.

matures, the cyclist evolves through experiences of competition and training. What may have been useful at one stage or phase of preparation may no longer be useful, or may be of less use at a later phase. Things change. For example, a novice entering a big race may be extremely excited with the challenge to perform. To manage their anxiety they may need to relax and define a pre-race structure to calm themselves and get into their optimal arousal zone.

After the same person has ridden for several years, what had once been very exciting may be experienced as just another race. Now instead of calming down, what the same individual may have to do is pump themselves up to get into that optimal zone.

Peg's example of what she calls "procrastination" illustrates this point:

PEG As I gained more experience and confidence in bike racing, I learned to procrastinate more. Yes, procrastinate. I could wait closer to start time before planning my strategy. That way, I was more accurate with the conditions such as weather, terrain, course changes, who I was racing and how I was feeling. Then I could focus more on my plan A and some on plan B, rather than having to plan out many scenarios without knowing what I might encounter. Having the extra pressure made me focus more, concentrate harder and worry less. I had more experiences to draw on, although I learned something new each race. Being open to that challenge made it exciting instead of foreboding.

It is also interesting to note that your pre-race routine and personality profile can change. I never thought I'd see the day when I wouldn't be nervous for a race. Eventually, it happened. I had to develop new routines to motivate myself. I needed to pump up more before a race than to calm down. To do that, I exaggerated the importance of events or mentally inflated the prize money to get myself more excited. I found that I didn't need to be alone as much before races, I could warm-up with a teammate. I think I was lucky to have good coaches and team managers who allowed me the space when

I needed it and allowed me to change when the time came.

Getting perspective:

Where are you in terms of the skills you want to develop?

_____

Where are you in regard to training habits?

_____

What kind of attitude do you have in terms of commitment, confidence, identity and beliefs?

_____

Where are you in regard to your season?

_____

And where are you in regard to your career?

_____

Cathy was a talented mountain biker. I had watched her improve at training camps each year. One day, she called for some advice. She had just returned from a series of races in Europe where she had ridden very well. She said she was disappointed because she had a couple of mediocre performances since returning to North America. I explained to her that she wasn't a machine that could just be turned on and "go" full out, continuously. Rather, she was a human being. And, after an aggressive and successful tour in Europe, what she needed to do was cut herself a little slack, reduce the expectation and give herself a few easy weeks. Then build back her competitive edge. An important part of being a professional cyclist is learning how to manage and pace your peaks. Giving yourself permission to rest and recharge is essential to that process.

Cathy acknowledged her need for a rest, as well as her impatience. As we spoke, she confided that she had decided it was time to make a significant shift from being on the edge of the world's top 10, to consistently being in the top four to eight. "Sounds great," I said. Then I asked, "What has to change in the way you ride for you to make the shift?"

She was quiet.

"Is it skill?" I asked.

"No," she replied, "my skills are adequate."

"Is it conditioning?"

"No," she said again.

"Then, what is it?" I asked.

She thought for a moment, then said, "It's pace. I go out too slow. I seem to be saving myself for the final lap."

"Well," I replied, "that's reasonable. It's reasonable to pace yourself so you have something left for the end. However, if you want to be one of the best in the world you have to go beyond reason. You have to be more aggressive on the first three laps.

"You have to be 'unreasonable' like a cougar or a mountain lion."

I made her a tape to remind her to focus on her breathing, and to use her power words and images. And she consistently started to ride in the top 10. Needless to say, a better rested and "less reasonable" Cathy was eighth at the world championships.

PEG I had success very early in my career, making the

National Development Team after only one season of racing, and winning a bronze medal my very first time at the world championships. This put me at a certain level with expectations of results to match.

I've seen this pattern many times with talented young riders who want to achieve results quickly, when it can take years to master figuring out your own peaking schedule, tactics and equipment needs. The key here is patience and gaining perspective. Everyone is different and on their own time schedule for reaching the pinnacle of their cycling career. Some will take longer than others, but may have a longer, more fruitful career as a result. The good news is that it doesn't seem to matter what age you start at, just give yourself time. Racers like Linda Jackson and Ned Overend began in their 30s but had talent and commitment, and excelled, in spite of their relatively late starts.

A shift in perspective, even if it seems relatively unimportant, can sometimes alter your feelings and enhance your performance.

PEG Sometimes getting more information or a different perspective can lighten pressure. I used to feel some additional pressure at races if I had been interviewed prior to the event. It wasn't until years later that I finally asked a reporter if it mattered how the athlete who had been interviewed actually performed. She replied, "Not really." She went on to say that readers are impressed by what the racer is attempting, and results are rarely as important as publicizing the upcoming event. Hmm, if only I had asked back then, I might have felt more support instead of more pressure. With less focus on others' expectation and a greater sense of support I would have ridden even better.

When I was on the Weight Watcher's Frozen Foods Team, we were given media training. We practiced interviews and watched ourselves on videotape. I enjoyed the media challenge and the experience made me more aware of our team image. The image we portrayed was more important to the sponsors than our race results. As a very task-oriented person that seemed strange, but knowing this helped me to grow a broader perspective on the whole racing scene. I still prepared for races to the best of my ability, but the pressure to perform was reduced with the knowledge that how the team promoted the product was equally as important. I became more adaptable at events and happier with my results.

Another example of perspective shift occurred prior to my first world championship road race. I was nervous and met with the U.S. National Team sport psychologist, Andy Jacobs. We did some relaxation and visualization, and then he asked me, "What can you change right now in this situation that will help you to perform?" I knew the answer and replied, "Just my attitude." In this case, it was important not to dwell on the outcome, the dream of finishing first and becoming world champion, but to focus on the task at hand—completing the road race to the best of my ability.

Pressure is always there. When you are confronted with pressure "use it." Use it as a cue or reminder to breathe and refocus—but refocus on what? You can refocus on the thoughts and images that give you power, on thoughts and images that give you the feeling that you want to have, and on thoughts and images you've had on days when you really excelled.

When you experience pressure, choose to use it. It's your choice.

LIFESTYLE

Generally, when I address any high–performance group in sport or business I like to remind them that one thing that nurtures their continuous development and success is lifestyle. By lifestyle, I mean quite simply, the way we live. Generally, that relates to our diet, exercise, rest and recreation, relationships and attitude.

There are large individual differences among cyclists. We have already discussed personality differences. There are also significant physical differences. Cyclists come in all shapes, sizes, genders, colors and ages. In addition, there are different needs and preferences. Our lifestyle prescription has general comments in each of the five areas noted above.

DIET

There are many theories and fads about diet, and there are marked individual differences in performance needs.For instance, a sprinter or kilo racer, who only race for a minute or two, may have very different needs than a road racer who rides hard for several hours. Then there are individual differences in metabolism, culture, history and preference.

Because cycling is so demanding, many adult cyclists have developed a consciousness about how their performance is affected by what they eat. In general, most recommend and follow a diet rich in complex carbohydrates, high in fiber, low in fat, with a moderate amount of protein. Plenty of fluid is advised (see "Spot Check," chapter two[9]).

EXERCISE

Most cyclists get plenty of exercise.

But remember to have fun, balance activities and get some rest. People need time-outs. Schedule a day, a week or month off. You are not literally a machine.

REST AND RECREATION

Rest. It is essential to balance work and activity with rest and passivity. Rest is vital, and it should be quality rest. As the former U.S. national cycling coach Eddy B said, "When I say rest, I don't mean lying on the beach and drinking beer. When I say rest, I mean rest from the bike, not rest from training." It's a good idea to improve your quality rest and recreation skills by learning some relaxation or meditation techniques. Sleep is also very important. Just as you schedule training, get sufficient rest and meet your sleep needs.

Recreation means re-creation. The most common form of recreation in North America is television. TV is neither renewing nor recharging. So, balance passivity with activity, rest with action, habit with spontaneity, and do things that

---

[9] For more on the subject, see *Complete Guide to Sport Nutrition*, by Monique Ryan, Velo-Press, Boulder, CO. 1999.

are fun. For someone who sits at a desk all day, or is confined indoors, getting out on your bike is recreational, fun and a great balance. For someone who rides hours a day, just being still, doing something like meditation, can be recreational. Likewise with dancing, swimming, listening to music or going for a walk.

RELATIONSHIP

We are social animals. Whether you are introverted or extroverted, people- or task-oriented, the relationships you have with others are an important part of your life. For competitive cyclists who invest a great deal of their energy in training, they need some nurturing and supportive relationships both within cycling from coaches, teammates and training partners, as well as outside of cycling from loved ones—husbands, wives, lovers, parents and friends. If you do receive support from significant others, accept it. Then, remember to support them when you are not riding.

ATTITUDE

The attitude that we bring to any situation in life colors our experience. We talked about an optimal cycling attitude—commitment, confidence and identity—in chapter five. Three elements of attitude that are helpful to bring to your daily life are courage, gratitude and love.

Courage is the heart to set life goals that challenge you and the heart to work toward meeting these goals.

Gratitude is the appreciation of what you have, not what's missing. Many cyclists know of some other people, including cyclists who were tragically injured riding their bicycles, who are ill, even paralyzed, and are unable to get out in the fresh air and go for a walk or ride a bike. Don't sweat the small stuff. Every day be grateful for your health and energy and the opportunity and potential to make today a special day.

Love is having the heart to embrace the people and opportunities in your life, to be kind, positive, and to treat others as you would like to be treated.

PEG Having taken coaching courses while I was racing, I was aware of many of the lifestyle issues that Saul just mentioned. However, as a performer, I was so involved that it was sometimes difficult to maintain an objective perspective and see when I was getting off-track or when I needed more rest. My personal coach, Len Goodman, was usually able to point out those things to me and remind me, even though I already knew the information and the signs.

Now, as a coach, I often ask spouses, parents and training partners for input on how the athlete is doing in relationships, eating patterns and attitude. It helps both coach and athlete to get outside feedback.

HOMEWORK

1. Whether you are a rider or a coach, determine which of the following attributes best describes your cycle-psyche style. Are you more introverted or extroverted? More feeling- or task-oriented? More detailed specific or more of a generalizer? And what impact does this have on your training and pre-race patterns?

PEG MAASS HILL

ROBERT MAJOR

COME TO THE START LINE WITH THE CONFIDENCE THAT YOU ARE PREPARED
PHYSICALLY, HAVE SKILL COMPETENCY AND ARE MENTALLY READY FOR
THE CHALLENGE. YOUR STRATEGY REFLECTS YOUR UNIQUENESS.

If you want to explore this subject more fully, or if you want to take the complete Myers Briggs Type Inventory, see a sport psychologist.

2. Compare your Pre-Competition Schedule with that of a teammate or friend you travel with to cycling events. Discuss differences and how to make allowances for each person's performance needs to be met.

3. In your journal, write down any changes that you observe yourself beginning to make in your pre-race or race routines as a function of your growing awareness of your "type." It's said that it takes doing something 11 times to make it a new habit.

HOMEWORK REVIEW

FROM THE EIGHT RIDERS:

1. PEG At the sessions, a sense of "deserving" struck a cord with several under-confident riders. They had been focusing on training as if that were the sole answer. "If I train more I will race better." That was the belief. However, physical fitness was not their downfall.

In one case, skills and awareness were lacking. In another case, negative self-talk and fear of crashing held a rider back from performing the way he deserved. We made plans to address these flaws. As the riders saw some improvement in these areas, it gave them pleasure, more confidence and a new feeling of having control over their performance.

2. During the session, several riders said that they felt that they were being described in the various personality sketches: "Sounds like me." They had fun relaying stories of their personality responses in various race situations. There were parts of race routines that will be forever changed. For example, two riders missed their warm-up by spending so much time looking for a toilet before the start. They now check out toileting details in advance.

3. Once again, it will take time for each rider to sort out their ideal race routine, but the forms appear to give them a good head start. They got ideas from each other about warming up and things to pack. I noticed that few bring a towel and wash cloth for after races, to wipe down before putting on dry clothes. I gave them my wipe-down formula of one-quarter witch hazel and three-quarters rubbing alcohol. A blanket has many uses—as a screen to change behind, keep warm in nasty weather, and to cushion bikes and wheels in the car.

In a follow-up session, we took another look at race strategy. This expanded on the observations of the demands of each discipline, by analyzing the demands of specific courses. We could use our visualization skills and training diary notes to recall specifics about courses—how long climbs were, direction of prevailing winds, gears used, distance from the last turn to the finish line, all the crucial elements of the course. I also asked how the course was typically won, where the winning move was made, how far into the race, by an individual or a group? This was not to say that it couldn't be won another way, but it helped to establish the crucial elements and moves.

The next step was to compare the racer's strengths and weaknesses with the specific demands of that course. Again, the racers were proficient at that. An easy way of finding out what you are good at, is to note what things you like doing in training or racing. Athletes usually prefer to do things they are good at, and dislike things they are not good at. It was fun to map out strategy focusing on the things at which a rider excelled. With these possibilities in mind, the athletes could then visualize the upcoming race with more clarity and focus on their tasks than before.

To summarize:

- Evaluate the demands of the course—physically, mentally, tactically.
- Answer how it has been won in the past, and what your strengths and weaknesses are in comparison.
- Form strategies to use your strengths and minimize your weaknesses.
- Use positive self-affirmations to keep focused on your strengths, and follow your plan.
- Repeat this process for each event, building your experience and ability to read races.

SPOT CHECK: NEW EQUIPMENT

PEG It is so tempting for riders to try new equipment, as if it is an immediate shortcut to better performance. In some cases, the innovations are real. Take Graham Obree's pursuit bike and new Superman position that rocked the world championships or the Italian team time trial squad that used belts secured to their top tubes for more leverage, or the first skin suit.... Cycling is a highly technical sport. However, those who use technology successfully are usually well practiced with the new product. It is also a rule of thumb to make changes before June, so you have time to get accustomed to the change prior to important events of the late summer.

My team mechanic took the risk of installing tri-bars on my pursuit bike for my last year at the U.S. nationals, without asking me first. I had been using the bars extensively in road time trialing, so I was excited when he brought out the "surprise." I liked the idea of being the first American to use them at the track nationals. It wasn't much of a risk due to my familiarity with the handlebars and knowing that I liked to be innovative.

This approach failed for Rebecca Twigg at the 1996 Olympics. In a *VeloNews* article following the Olympics, she said that her unfamiliarity with a new pursuit bike hurt her performance in Atlanta. Make sure you do your homework before using a new piece of equipment or new position at your big event—the same can be said for making changes with food and beverages.

There's a tendency to feel vulnerable and intimidated when the competition is sporting the latest technical innovations, flashy equipment, ultralight frames or aerodynamic wheels. Remember, the productive choice is to "use it" and keep spinning the wheel. Focus on your situation, and remind yourself that you are prepared and will perform to the best of your ability with the equipment you have. Use affirmations to remind yourself that you can rise to the challenge. Choose to have confidence in your own preparation. You can handle it. It is the human body that drives the machines, and you can use the challenge to be pushed to be your best.

Use it, or it uses you. Remember, confidence comes from

your preparation with the equipment you practiced with. I like the expression, "Do it where you are, with what you have."

Keep
spinning
the wheel

"At the beginning stages, it is definitely the total physical development that is important. Later on, you develop more mental concentration, mental preparation to maintain the physical capacity. Next, you develop the spiritual."

—Eddy Merckx[10]

T he goal of chapter eight is to look at mental toughness as an integral part of many of the training elements presented in the first seven chapters. It's to provide feedback of cyclists and coaches reviewing the training process, and to discuss cycling as a spiritual exercise and an opportunity for personal development.

STRATEGY AND MENTAL TOUGHNESS

A s we move into our final chapter, let's review two concepts: strategy and mental toughness. We discussed strategy in chapter six. Usually it's seen as a "game plan," a way to ride a race. It's a mental competence. The strategy one

[10] *The Quotable Cyclist*, edited by Bill Strickland, Breakaway Books, New York, 1997.

chooses is really an integration of many things. It is based on the rider's fitness level, attitude, style, bike-handling skills, the type and difficulty of the course, the weather, and, quite possibly, the other cyclists in the race.

I discussed strategy with a world-class mountain biker. She thought maybe I was overemphasizing the importance of strategy. She said, "My own strategy is fairly simple. I go off hard on the first lap, and get a good line. I'm a little below max on the second lap, I pick it up for the third and 'blast it,' and give it everything I have left in the last lap." I asked her if it was really that straightforward and consistent.

"That's it," she replied. After a moment she added, "Well, I guess there is some variability to my strategy. Late in the season, when my fitness level is at a peak, my skill sets are sharp, and my confidence is high, I'm more aggressive. I feel stronger. There are many more situations where I attack than I would earlier in the season."

As we said in chapter one, our feelings affect our thinking, and our thinking shapes how we ride. Strategy is an integration, and like all complex cycling judgments it's affected as much by how you manage thoughts and feelings as it is by your physical fitness and the challenge of the course.

The same can be said about mental toughness.[11] Most cyclists would agree that competitive cycling is a sport that demands mental toughness. There are many obstacles and barriers to distract riders and racers as they push themselves to the limits.

[11] For a comprehensive discussion of mental toughness see: *The New Toughness Training For Sports*, James E. Lohrer, PLUME/Penguin, New York, London, 1995.

Mental toughness is the ability to maintain focus on what you want to create, no matter what. It's an integration of many things discussed in the training program. Mental toughness has to do with motivation, with knowing what you want to achieve and having the desire to excel. It's about commitment and the willingness to do what's necessary to achieve that goal. It's about knowing what to do and having clear focus. It's about emotional control, thinking positively, and not allowing yourself to be distracted or limited by fear, pain and difficulty. Like all attitudinal factors, mental toughness has a psycho-physical dimension that brings us back to the basics of breathing and focus.

Vince Lombardi, the legendary football coach, said that fatigue can make cowards of almost anyone. When most people experience fatigue and pain they stop what they are doing and rest.

When a mentally tough bicycle racer experiences fatigue or pain in a race, they use it to spin the wheel, or they ignore it.

When most people experience frustration and difficulty, they tense up and slow down.

When a committed bicycle rider experiences frustration and difficulty, they use it.

When most people experience distracting and irrelevant thoughts, their attention drifts and their productivity diminishes.

When a mentally tough cyclist experiences distracting and irrelevant thoughts, which can sometimes happen for physiological reasons, such as when people fatigue and experience oxygen deficits, it can be harder to concentrate. They use it to recharge and refocus—and performance surges.

The mind is amazing. It can think about fear, pain, anger, fatigue, difficulty or irrelevant thoughts. Mental toughness is knowing how to release these limiting thoughts. It's about being aware of your direction and staying tuned in. As we said earlier, winners experience fear, doubt and uncertainty. They just don't focus on or hold these feelings. They use them to spin the wheel, and refocus on the power elements.

EXERCISE NO. 1: STAYING FOCUSED

Select a simple scenario to imagine, like time trialing. As you begin to make a mental image of this, check the time or start a stopwatch. When you lose focus for longer than a few seconds, stop and check the time to see how long you were able to stay focused. This exercise is repeatable. After regular practice, time yourself again, and you will see improvement. Remaining focused is a skill that can be learned and improved.

Mental toughness isn't magic or a miracle. It's about staying focused on what you love and what you want to create. When people are able to do that, amazing things are possible. Creative thought and love are two of the most powerful forces at our disposal.

There's the story about a cyclist who had trouble focusing. It seemed his mind always wandered, even in races. It became enough of a problem that he sought the counsel of a number of his friends. One of his mates suggested that he go see this "guru" who was supposed to be an expert in teaching people how to still the mind. After meeting the cyclist, the guru suggested that the young man sit quietly for two hours each day and just focus on his breathing. The young man followed the guru's advice diligently for a couple of weeks, but he was still plagued by wandering thoughts, most of which were about sex. So, the cyclist went back to the guru and explained his dilemma. The old man smiled, "That's not a problem. Thinking about sex is understandable for a healthy young man like you." Then, raising his voice he cautioned the cyclist, "But whatever you do, don't think about monkeys."

"Monkeys?" replied the young man incredulously. "I never think about monkeys."

So, he went back to his room, sat down to focus on his breathing and he began to think of…monkeys.

The mind does play tricks. The mind is always on. It's there to scan your world and keep you safe. Yet, it may do things to distract you and draw you away from your focus. Indeed, sometimes—like in the above story—the mind will focus on the very thing we are asking it to avoid. Part of competency is mastering the mind. Part of mastering the mind is your ability to stay focused.

I was talking to a group of cyclists and triathletes. They were a mix of competitive, recreational and developmental cyclists. I had basically given them "the course" on sport psychology. We had talked about breathing for emotional control and power, about power thoughts, affirmations and power imagery. Then, one woman who had asked some questions earlier posed an interesting question, one that many riders have had.

She asked, "When I am descending fast the thought sometimes pops into my mind that I am going too fast and that I could crash. When that happens I become tense and slow right down. I just can't seem to get that negative thought out of my mind. Is there something you could recommend?"

What makes the story even more interesting is that when we were discussing animal imagery earlier in the course most of the group picked the big cats, tigers, panthers, cheetahs and mountain lions for their performance-enhancing image. A few of the group picked eagles, wolves and racing dogs such as greyhounds. When I asked this woman what animal image might give her qualities that would enhance her performance she said, "a dog."

When I further inquired as to what kind of dog she was imaging, she replied, "My cocker spaniel. I like to run and ride with my cocker spaniel." I acknowledged her remark at the time without commenting on it, but now that she was asking for advice about descending with speed, I said, "You are an intelligent and sensitive woman, and you have an active mind. The thoughts you are having are simply your mind trying to protect you, and running an anxious thought program. What I suggest is that whenever you experience fear or anxiety, go back to your breathing, release and breathe, and that will clear the TV screen. Then, say something to yourself that is calming and integrating. An excellent word for you is 'smooth.' And if you really want to descend with speed, then along with your breathing and that power thought, I recommend that you introduce the image of a descent specialist, an image like a mountain lion, an animal with incredible agility and balance."

I went on to tell her, "What you have done by choosing your cocker spaniel is to select something convenient and comfortable as a high-performance image. Clearly, you have a need for comfort. And while a part of you wants to descend with speed there is another part that wants to be safe and comforted. I can't tell you what you should do. However, if you genuinely want to descend with speed, then the cocker spaniel image has got to go."

The story is interesting for several reasons. First, it raises a problem many cyclists have about intrusive, limiting thoughts. Second, it reviews the importance of the basics like breathing, power thoughts and images in dealing with performance "issues." And third, it illustrates how cycling can be like a mirror that reflects some of our ongoing and unresolved uncertainties and imbalances. As such, cycling is stimulating, challenging, therapeutic and recreational.

Some people equate mental toughness with rigidity— being made of steel. I would like to remind those people of an ancient Oriental maxim that says he who is rigid breaks, while he who is flexible bends. Peg's mental toughness story that follows isn't about being inflexible, it is about staying on purpose and in the moment. Mental mastery doesn't mean negative thoughts and worries don't come to mind, it's just that you can handle them more quickly by being flexible, refocusing, and using all your tools.

PEG My mastery of problem solving became apparent one day while racing the Tour de L'Aude in France. For years, I had a recurring problem with tensing up when I heard gravel crunching underneath my tires. It bothered me ever since I had slipped and crashed on gravel, requiring stitches in my head. Now I heard that sound as we reached the top of a long, arduous climb. It was raining at the precipice, spray from the tires contributing to my demise. Other racers passed me as I hesitated. I could see the cow-path of a course ahead, descending a devious route into a wind-swept field. I knew that if I didn't get over this soon, I'd be off the back and chasing in no time.

After breathing and relaxing my shoulders and arms, I decided to find something to like or something positive about this water in my face. When would I appreciate that kind of misting and splashing?

The answer came to me: in a boat—the ocean spray off the bow of a boat, sailing with my dad in the summer. I could see the colorful jerseys in front of me turning on a switchback like full spinnaker sails on boats reaching for the next mark. Their bare, brown arms holding the handlebars reminded me of wind surfers. Yeah, that's what I was doing, wind surfing on a warm summer day, and loving it. I was back in the race after problem-solving on the fly.

I knew that I had really mastered the mental side of racing that day, when I was able to correct negative thoughts and feelings without having anticipated or rehearsed the scene before.

EXERCISE NO. 2: ADAPTING

This exercise will require the help of another cyclist or coach. While you are imaging a cycling scenario, they are to suggest a sudden change, like getting a flat tire, a surprise attack, or it begins to rain. Your task is to respond to the change in your image by managing feelings and using mental skills to remain focused on the performance task at hand.

FINAL FEEDBACK:
A FEW COMMENTS FROM THE FIELD

I often conclude training or therapy programs by asking the participants to provide feedback on the process. So, please reflect on the past seven chapters of input and training. As you were unable to communicate with us at the time of writing this book, we have asked several elite cyclists, international racers and cycling coaches, plus some of the riders Peg coaches, to comment on the sport psychology for cycling program. We also asked them to share with us some of their experiences of the material in the book and their experiences of cycling.

CHAPTERS ONE AND TWO

We began the training process with a description of how the mind works and how to use breathing to create feelings of rhythm and ease.

All of the cyclists and coaches who reviewed the chapter liked the metaphor of the mind as a TV set. They felt, as we do, that it is simple, easy to understand and most importantly, puts responsibility for managing the mind clearly on the shoulders of the cyclist.

While everyone agreed that breathing is critical to psycho-physical control, there was some question as to whether we should have introduced the breathing training in chapter one or later in the book. Dr. Miller's feeling is that breathing is key and everyone is a breather. Working with breathing is a fast and effective way to "change channels," that is, to change feeling and focus. Besides, that's how he conducts the training, so we presented it that way in the book.

Several riders and coaches said, "If you don't simply read through the first two chapters, but actually spend time experiencing the processes, then these chapters, indeed the whole program, is really beneficial."

CHAPTERS THREE AND FOUR

This is the "stuff" that people tend to think about when they think of sport psychology, and these two chapters on programming were very popular. The feedback was that the information was useful and the chapters were fun to read.

The feedback from most cyclists was that these chapters reminded them that they should be more constructively positive in their thinking. One said, "I hadn't thought about lining up so many positive things to say to myself." Another rider said, "I didn't appreciate there being a big difference between thinking, 'I'm going to win,' and 'I better win,' but if, as you suggest, I were to visualize myself riding with these two thoughts, I can feel the difference between the two. The image of 'I'm going to win' is powerful. The image of 'I'd better win,' is fearful. From now on, I'm going to be more aware and more positive in the way I talk to myself."

The words "attack" and "smooth" seemed to give people a good way to stay alert and conceptualize how to use their energy in a race. People liked many of the affirmations. Another rider commented, "Affirmations work, especially if I use the breathing first, to get a positive feeling before repeating an affirmation. In the past, I have repeated some affirmations, but they weren't as believable without the feelings."

Some riders felt the chapter presented too many affirmations; kind of like a power thought supermarket. We wanted to express a range of what is possible and effective in power thinking, and make it clear that power thoughts can relate to technical and strategical things as well as self-image and self-esteem issues. We also want to use that input to remind you that six to eight power thoughts is not only enough, it's ideal.

Regarding power imagery, most of the cyclists who provided some feedback said that they use(d) some form of mental rehearsal. And, judging from the feedback, will do so more aggressively in the future.

The animal imagery—stimulating images—was very popular with people. It provides simple license and easy access to the power stored in our animal spirit. Most cyclists, like most athletes, select the big cats as power images seemingly because of their speed, balance, power and beauty. Wolves and eagles were also popular.

CHAPTER FIVE

The greatest interest in chapter five on attitude, seemed to be in regard to confidence. While most people acknowledged that success, in the form of race results, builds confidence far fewer seemed to appreciate that success with the specific training elements could also grow confidence. It's a point we think is important and something we underlined in our discussion of competence in chapter six. The information most people reportedly "got" from the chapter was that a winning attitude doesn't simply happen in a vacuum without doing the work. Creating positive feelings with breathing and release techniques, thinking positive thoughts, visualizing positive images, and doing the physical training are the building blocks of confidence, a positive identity, and a sense of deserving.

The commitment idea of "using it" was seen as a practical way to stay positively focused. Indeed, one Olympic and world championship medalist responded to our advice, "Always use your situation or feeling to remind you to spin the wheel," with the pun, "That's a great way to put a positive spin on a bad situation."

Chapter Six

In chapter six, several riders mentioned that they enjoyed reading about all the elements that went into becoming competent in their event(s) and in the different cycling specialities. One rider said, "When I actually saw all the elements I have mastered, it made me realize how good I am at my event." This is something we discussed throughout the book. Many riders commented that they are more aware of confidence coming from physical training, skills and mental preparation.

A rider shared, "I used to get my confidence just from my race results. Now I can get confidence from completing a workout, riding single-track well or from planning my race strategy."

One aspect of the program that several riders seemed to appreciate was that it highlighted the variety and diversity of elements required by the many different cycling specialties. Some riders said that made them more aware of the uniqueness of their event. Others said they enjoyed learning things about other cycling specialties that, frankly, they wouldn't have bothered to read about if there were a separate section on that other specialty.

CHAPTER SEVEN

Many cyclists reported that they found the information on individual differences in chapter seven very interesting. The consensus was that they hadn't thought a great deal about how personality "style" could make a difference on how they, or others, prepared and competed. However, many people said they could identify qualities about themselves in this chapter saying, "Yeah, that's me" and gained some insight about their "style" that they would put to use in their preparation and racing. One rider said, "I guess I'm an internally focused individual because when you said 'eyes' I thought of looking inward and checking out how I felt. And, when I thought of others, I thought of them looking at me. Up until now, I hadn't thought so much of scanning them."

One of the clearest illustrations of individual differences I experienced occurred at a meeting with a group of elite cross-country mountain bikers. One cyclist, an Olympian and World Cup veteran—an extroverted, externally oriented, feeling-oriented generalizer—commented on how he used his competitors in the race to "psyche himself up" and to bring out his best. Another cyclist, a world champion—a more internally focused, task-oriented, introvert—said, "I never do that. I don't focus on them at all. I break the race into sections and focus on achieving perfection in each section."

Many riders approved of the competition sheets and asked if they could copy them. We have put templates of these forms that can be copied in Appendix D.

CONCLUSION

Sport is a metaphor of life. This is nowhere more evident than in the sport of cycling.

Cycling is a psycho-physical adventure. It presents a dynamic challenge that can awaken in each rider the human spirit for excitement, competition and survival. In optimal cycling the rider must push him- or herself to the maximum, and to a place where they will inevitably face their vulnerability, in the form of fear, pain and difficulty. Facing this challenge alone, and sometimes in cold, wet and tired moments, a cyclist can come to know him- or herself better, and their personal sense of confidence grows.

"When the spirits are low, when the day appears dark, when the work becomes monotonous, when hope hardly seems worth having, just mount a bicycle and go for a spin down the road, without thought of anything but the ride you are taking."

—Arthur Conan Doyle,
author of Sherlock Holmes *mysteries*

One tribe of Native Americans had an expression "turning the wheel" for those times in life when people face a real-life challenge and meet the test. Optimal cycling can provide that challenge and that test. In more ways than one, cycling affords us an opportunity to "turn the wheel."

Cycling isn't simply sweat and grind. It can also be recreational.

Recently, I went to the World Cup of field hockey as part of Canada's men's team. Like any world championship, the World Cup was an extremely competitive forum. This one was held in the Netherlands, a flat green country where millions of people ride bicycles. The competing teams stayed in a recreational retreat situated in the countryside about 30 miles from Utrecht. Each team was housed in several cottages, and each cottage was provided with a bicycle for the use of its inhabitants. It was the standard model-T unit, single speed.

Every morning, I would get up early and take our bicycle for a 40-minute ride along the dikes. In this quiet, solitary time I was able to pedal away from the competitive swirl of the event and experience a different perspective. It was like a meditation. It was recharging. Indeed, it was true recreation, and it became a healthy, balancing way to begin a productive, high-pressure day.

PEG The night before a big race that I had really focused on, I would ride in my street clothes through neighborhoods. I could see in their windows, families sitting down to dinner, their weekend chores done, the lawn nicely mowed. It reminded me that life goes on, that my performance in tomorrow's race wasn't so crucial. It helped me keep things in perspective and to be more relaxed.

EXERCISE NO. 3:
DRAW YOUR BIKE. SEE IT, FEEL IT, DRAW IT...

A bicycle is an amazing machine. Some cyclists see it as just that, a machine. Others see it as a horse to ride or race—a winged horse. Some see their bikes as an escape mechanism that can take them away from the stress and pressures of everyday life. Here's a fun exercise. Try it, even if you don't like to draw.

Place your bicycle where you can look at it. Get comfortable, and then draw your bicycle. Drawing it forces you to really look at it, in ways that you may not have looked at it before. Draw all the parts, draw the proportion, and draw the way it makes you feel. Then, select six adjectives to describe your bicycle.

A friend of mine painted a picture of her bicycle, which she really loved. It's one of my favorite pictures.

"MY BIKE," PAINTING AND PHOTO BY SUE KERR

Cycling can be a spiritual adventure. As I said in chapter five discussing commitment, cycling is a dharma, a path to self-realization. Any discipline that draws us to it and allows us to invest our being, and helps us to grow, can become such a path. Cycling does that.

In chapter five we also said that people have two sides or natures. We are animals and angels. As animals we compete and survive in a very physical reality. It is a world of body, speed and power. Cycling challenges the animal in us. Using some of the animal identity images discussed in chapter four, you can tap this energy and give yourself more power to compete and excel.

People are also angels. We have the remarkable gift through thought and imagination to create our reality. Cycling nurtures that spiritual side of us. Anyone can jump on their bicycle and pedal to another place. A place where they are lighter and freer to experience themselves in a brighter light.

Balance is a key to well-being. Cycling can nurture both our competitive, physical, animal nature and our cerebral, spiritual, creative side.

At the beginning of the book, we highlighted the importance of breathing both for generating power and for emotional control. Let's end our training with the breath. The Greek word psyche originally meant "the breath," as in life's breath or the spirit of life. Cycling can move us into the world of breath and spirit. As such it can be an inspiring, transformative and enlightening pastime.

As you ride through life remember to breathe—and spin the wheel.

HOMEWORK

1. Review the book and your journal notes to see how you have grown and changed with your new information, awareness, skill and confidence.

HOMEWORK REVIEW

The athletes we worked with were able to discuss and debrief after each chapter.

SPOT CHECK: SEEING THE WHOLE

There are several hindrances to seeing the whole. Here are three examples.

1. I was talking with an athlete the other day who said that he notices when he rides he sometimes develops a kind of tunnel vision and locks onto a limited perspective of what is right in front of him. He asked me for a simple response that he could use to get rid of his tunnel vision. Essentially, what I recommended was a simple mechanical response that involves raising the eyebrows and opening the eyes wide in an exaggerated way, and then taking a breath. This simple response appears to break the tension lock that is a part of tunnel vision.

2. Recently, I was talking with an athlete who was experiencing another aspect of limited vision. She was having a couple of difficult days. She had had a spill that resulted in her having to take a few days off the bike to rehab. She was a committed, hard-working athlete and was concerned and upset that missing a couple of days training on her bike was going to upset her training schedule and compromise her season.

One of her teammates on the national team suggested she see me. I listened to her vent and understood something of her frustration. I suggested to her that if life gives you lemons you had better make lemonade. I explained that she had a good aerobic base, was very fit and that losing four or five days riding wasn't going to make a significant difference to her season. I suggested that she use the time to work on her mental training—something she had not addressed very thoroughly. I suggested that we use her time off the bike to create a one-week mental training camp during which we would work on her breathing and define some power thoughts and sharpen her performance imagery as well as her attitude. We did some psychological testing, looked at her personality style and made adjustments to her preparation process. When she returned to her bike eight days later she was refreshed by her "week off" and motivated to ride. By her own admission, she was also much more aware of how to manage her thoughts and feelings to be a "better cyclist." She said, "It's funny how we can sometimes turn something bad into something good if we just change our thinking." "Yeah," I replied, "It's just a matter of seeing the whole, and choosing the part you've got as the good part."

3. Some time ago, I recall talking to an athlete who was very upset about not being selected for the Olympic team. He had trained hard and done almost everything to make the team, but, in the end, others out-performed him and he wasn't selected.

His disappointment was great. In trying to be supportive all I could think to say was, "If you give something your best shot, and it doesn't happen, it may be wise to accept that it wasn't meant to be. It's as if there were some other lesson you were meant to learn, or some other thing you were supposed to be doing."

I know from my personal experience that that response often doesn't seem to be very satisfying in those hurting moments; however, there is truth in knowing that some of the whole can only be seen, later, with faith and integrity.

APPENDIX A

JOURNAL NOTES

Week one

It feels good to be practicing the breathing and relaxation exercises again. I feel rusty on tuning in to myself. I'm not sure that the breath as a wheel idea works for me, but I will keep practicing it. The sound effects are motivating and fun. I like audio-visualizing the sound of a steam engine getting up to speed, and maintaining the rhythm.

This journal entry shows the cyclist is practicing, but is unsure of the skills. It takes time for each person to assimilate new techniques and to make them their own. Changing behaviors and thought patterns takes training, just like improving a physical component like climbing takes training.

Week two

Still working on the breathing. It's sometimes hard to remember when I'm also working on riding technique and trying to do harder efforts. It's almost like I go to the breathing too late. I'll try starting the effort with breathing, generating from the hips. I'm glad Saul mentioned about the chakra points—I have very strong energy sources just below my waist and I think in the mid-chest. I am going to remember to tune into these power points.

The breathe like a wheel reminds me of the rowing ergometer at the gym. It makes noise when you pull on the bar attached to the chain and flywheel. It's noisier and sounds more powerful when I pull harder and faster. It slows down in a steady manner, too. I can use that imagery and enrich it with the sound effects when I focus on my breathing.

Again, practice makes perfect. "Talking" things out in the journal allows the rider to problem solve and generate new ideas like "I'll try starting the effort with breathing." Drawing on past experiences like the sound of the rowing ergometer is useful and powerful because they are already imprinted in the mind. It makes the image personal and more comfortable. The athlete may like owning an original idea because it gives them the sense of having something—an edge that no one else has. The rider is also tuning into sounds. This is something she may not have been aware of before, so these exercises are opening up some exciting options to help her focus and be motivated.

WEEK THREE

Power words are a good start for me. They are reminding me of more detailed imagery and of identifying myself as an athlete. The words like "smooth" and "attack" help me to get into the moment more and be the top racer again. They also trigger other ideas I've used in the past like Ali's "float like a butterfly, sting like a bee." It's more playful again.

The breathing is starting to kick in, as is being patient with powering on climbs. I wish I had done more of the lower heart-rate work in the past. I think I overtrained the high end, keeping up with others when I should have trained my on-the-bike strength base more. Feels good to be doing it right now. I have more confidence in achieving my long-term goal since visualizing long-term goals and focusing on enjoying the moment instead of being critical and impatient.

I noticed today while running that when I got tired I was doing a three-step rhythm—left, right, left. I corrected it back to a four-beat left, right, left, right...added my breathing to the rhythm, and got smoother and faster.

The use of power words is giving the cyclist a new focus. Instead of negative self-talk there are positive action words. This is making sport more fun. She is also using competency knowledge to self-affirm. She knows that she is training in a more appropriate heart rate zone than in the past, and this knowledge gives her confidence and pleasure—"I'm doing the right thing." Her focus on long-term goals is sustaining her through this base work. She is definitely tuning into the sounds as shown by her observation of her running pattern, correcting from a three-beat to a four-beat gait. This also shows that she is more in the moment, observing her own actions during the run and correcting them. This is major progress.

WEEK FOUR

Working on imagery of racing. I don't seem to want to do too much detail—the unpleasant pain is not what I relish. I think I'm imaging how it is when I'm on top of things, not when I'm out of shape and suffering—that's reality. However, at least I'm focusing on the things I like about it, which keeps me going.

I learned in training camp how to (off-road) corner better on berms and loose terrain. It was really, really fun, and I know my skill level is greater than my confidence, but now I'm eager to try the tough trails again and not worry about what others think about my riding.

There is more self-analysis in this entry. She is looking more at the big picture and how the sport fits into her lifestyle. It's natural at this stage for some athletes to become introspective. Some question why they are in sports at all. She answers this with her notes of joy in learning a new skill and getting so much out of that. She loses her inhibitions such as caring what others think about her mountain-biking skills. She's finding what motivates her and gives her joy.

WEEK FIVE

I like the idea of knifing—using my aura. I need some pretty intense situations to try it, though. I could use it on the track, in pursuit, or chasing down someone. I'm not sure I can do much with it without a more intense, competitive situation.

I'm confused about my own attitude. I'm not sure what I want out of sport right now. I like to do things well. I like the feeling of confidence and speed. I work well under pressure, but how much pressure do I want? I've always thought that my identity is probably different in my own mind than how others perceive me. I think I can read a race extremely well and make moves. I'm not sure of my speed ability, but I did pretty well on the hill reps last night—slightly slower than last year, but not far off, and with significantly less effort. I have been focusing on pacing and staying within myself, which makes it more pleasant. I don't dread the workouts, and I know it is a better way to train, anyway. I will start off racing with the men until I feel fit enough to take on the women and expect to sprint at the end.

The comments here show willingness to try new ideas. She has had positive experiences after trying mental skills presented earlier in the book, and this makes it easier to work with new ideas. There are more questions concerning what she wants out of sport, a natural outcome of this process. She uses information from a workout to create confidence affirmations. She comes up with an idea to lessen pressure by riding with the men so there is no direct comparison with other women racers until she feels ready.

Week six

I'm being motivated by the competency idea. I have been using my heart rate monitor and aiming for the heart rate zone that I've heard is estimated lactate threshold (91-92 percent of max HR) and knowing that I would be holding that in a time trial. The longer I can keep in that zone, the more confident I get that I can race the length of time needed. It's rewarding that I can build that level up. First week I did a couple of minutes, now it's more like 30 minutes. I can use others to observe, and to cue myself to check my form. I'm not intimidated by how others perform. I focus on what I have to do out there. It's great to hear people encouraging each other. I'm excited about the athletes who have admitted their fears and are working on the skills they need—like Charlie doing that downhill corner 14 times until he got it.

This entry confirms that she has taken the idea of competency to gain confidence and notes use of the heart rate monitor for feedback. She is starting to focus more on the tasks she needs to do for a good performance in an upcoming race. She talks about using others as cues to keep her focused and seems to enjoy the camaraderie of others while going through this mental training camp.

WEEK SEVEN

I'm encouraged by reviewing the Meyers Briggs. I have grown, being more flexible in my introverted outlook. Compared to my early days of racing, I'm miles ahead, not thrown by small mistakes. Instead, I switch to plan B. Like on Sunday when I realized I had left my racing shoes at the last event. I just went to the other shoes. I had been thinking about trying them out again for my big April race anyway. It was nice to be calm about it. At the same time, I can stick to what I know works for me.

It has been good for me to train on my own more and to understand exactly what I'm doing—figuring out the times, how to get the reps in with the right amount of rest. I'm really pleased that I am getting more input. I've always needed to know why and how, and now I'm getting that again because I changed to what works for me instead of trying to please the coach by going to his workouts.

This athlete is a former national team cyclist, so she has past experiences to draw on. She gives an example of handling a stressful situation such as losing her racing shoes, by considering solutions instead of feeding into negative emotions. The confidence she gains from competency is very apparent now, and she is choosing to train alone and with specific knowledge to help feed that motivator.

WEEK EIGHT

I'm working on taking the good feelings I get from training on my own back into the group workout scenario. I know the group will push me more, I just have to take the good attitude in so I don't feel overly competitive or watched. I need to thank the others (in my mind) I train with before and after each interval, to feel like we are cooperating rather than competing. I haven't been able to visualize not being competitive with my training partners yet. I can do it with one person so far, and that's a good start. Especially because it is a person who yells "hello" just when I want to be invisible and go about my business without being noticed. I think it's hard for me to accept where I'm at, and that after all these years I still have to work hard. It doesn't come any easier even though I've paid my dues. I'm right back where I was 10 years ago, thinking about what I could change and what I couldn't. I know that all I can change is my attitude. I'm excited about being able to do the 100km randonneur event in two weekends—I've never had the chance to do a more low-key event, not a race. I'll learn from all of those who ride for the fun of it. Just like I re-learned from my new teammates more than 10 years ago what a cool sport this is.

This final entry shows that she has grown in self-knowledge during this process, but it is an ongoing process. Now that she knows herself better, she is ready to go back into the club setting with a stronger sense of what she needs and likes. She can use the group to contribute to her training. She has a more realistic perspective on herself and sees how sport fits into her life and how she is feeling about it. She is working on the things she can change.

WEEKS LATER

Had an awesome race today. I rode the course the day before, reviewing my strategy, visualizing the race. I determined time check points and met them. I was not pleased that we had a house guest for my big race, but he was forewarned that I don't like to talk in the morning while preparing. I pretty well ignored him, but I did what I had to do. On the course I was so focused, I used the pain to know I was on schedule. I even felt more social at the start because I was so confident about my preparation; I knew my training was good and that I could cover the distance in the time goal I set. I was physically peaked and felt good.

I used cue words like "flow" and "go" before going into the difficult sections. The hills didn't seem so tough because I was ready for them and knew them so well. I knew the last mile so well and surged with all I had. I felt like I was in the Zone.

Mission accomplished.

HIGH-PERFORMANCE CYCLIST'S PROFILE

PHYSICAL PERFORMANCE FACTORS	Cross-country mountain biking	Downhill mountain biking	Individual time trials	Stage races	Classic	Pursuit	Points race
Cycling-specific strength	very high	medium	medium	high	high	high	high
Speed	medium	high	medium	high	high	high	very high
Maximal anaerobic lactic power and anaerobic lactic capacity	medium	high	very low	high	high	medium	high
Maximal anaerobic lactic power and anaerobic lactic capacity	high	high	medium	very high	very high	very high*	very high
Maximal aerobic power (VO₂ max)	very high	high	very high*	very high	very high	very high	very high
Endurance capacity	very high	low	high	very high	very high	medium	high
Efficiency and skills	very high	very high	high	high	high	high	high
Body composition	very high	low	high	very high	very high	high	high
Flexibility	medium	high	medium	low	low	low	low
Capacity to repeat anaerobic efforts	very high	high	low	very high	very high	low	very high
Wellness management	nutrition, health care	nutrition, health care	nutrition, health care *for races with durations above 9 minutes	nutrition, health care	nutrition, health care	nutrition, health care *for races with durations below 5 minutes	nutrition, health care
Competitions							
Length of annual cycle	**7 months**	**6 months**	**8 months**	**8 months**	**8 months**	**8 months**	**8 months**
Number of competitions in annual cycle	50-60 (15-20 cross-country mountain biking)	20-25 (15-20 downhill mountain biking)	15-20	100-120	100-120	80-90 (10 pursuit)	80-90 (10 points race)
Training-to-competition ratio	4:1	6:1	8:1	2:1	2:1	12:1	12:1
Performance indicators	top-eight world's, World Cups, UCI rankings, nationals, CCA rankings	top-eight world's, World Cups, UCI rankings, nationals, CCA rankings	top-eight world's, ITT stages, nationals, average speed	qualify world's, win national tours, UCI rankings	top-eight world's, top-four World Cups, UCI rankings	top-eight world's, top-four World Cups, UCI rankings, time standards	top-eight world's, top-four World Cups, major games

Very high indicates what is considered the most important determinant(s) of performance.

APPENDIX C
TRAVEL TO COMPETITION

Event_____date_____start time _____

Wake-up   the alarm clock is set for_____
Wake-up routine   my wake-up plan is: (positive self-talk, smile,
                      waking-up feeling positive,
                      stretching, etc....)

                      _____

                      _____

                      _____
Visualize   my time for visualizing is:_____

Meals and meal plans
  (fill in those that apply, including snacks)
  breakfast   what:_____   time:_____
  lunch   what:_____   time:_____
  dinner   what:_____   time:_____

Activity   things I need to do before I leave:

                      _____

                      _____

                      _____
Rest   time for resting: from_____ to _____
Equipment check   when:_____
                      what to check:_____
Departure   departure time:_____
                      getting there (mode, route and with whom)

                      _____

                      _____

                      _____

                      Plan B:

                      _____

                      _____

                      _____

AT COMPETITION SITE

Event _____date _____start time _____

Parking, unloading plan: _____

Check race schedule, sign-in, adjust race plan accordingly

Recheck equipment   if it needs adjustment I will: _____

                               I will ask for help from: _____

Mentally rehearse   time:_____ place: _____

Competition strategy my strategy is: _____

                               start:_____

                               first 1/4: _____

                               second 1/4:_____

                               third 1/4: _____

                               finish: _____

                               checkpoints: _____

                               key parts of the course: _____

                               _____

Warm-up   time:_____ consisting of: _____

                               _____

Washroom breaks   time:_____ location: _____

Personal time   time:_____ to focus I will:_____

                               _____

                               to reduce stress I will:_____

                               _____

Centering   plan for checking mental state:_____

                               ways to refocus: _____

                               _____

Self-talk   self-talk, power words and thoughts for the race:

                               _____

                               _____

Imagery   images for the race:_____

                               _____

COMPETITION STRATEGY

Event information   the terrain: _____

format and rules: _____

weather conditions:_____

strengths and weaknesses of my opponents: __

_____

Personal strategy   my personal race plan is to: (Script it)

Evaluate strategy   during the event I will observe how the event is unfolding, compare with my strategy, and decide if I should continue as planned.

Options   my Plan B is: (Script it) _____
my Plan C is: (Script it) _____

Self-talk   my power words are: _____
my positive thoughts are: _____
my reasons for deserving to do my best are: __

_____

Technique   skills I focus on are: _____

Reducing tension   I scan my body and reduce tension by: _____

Handling pressure   at crucial times I think about: _____

Finish   before the finish I:_____

After the event, evaluate the appropriateness of your plan and follow-through. Pat yourself on the back for things well done.

I will continue to: _____

_____

I will correct the following:_____

_____

REFERENCES

1. Several quotes were taken with permission from *The Quotable Cyclist*, edited by Bill Strickland, Breakaway Books, New York, 1997

2. References on chakras:

Energy, Ecstasy and Your Seven Vital Chakras, Bernard Gunther, Newcastle Publishing, N. Hollywood, CA, 1983

The Chakras and The Human Energy Field, S. Kargulla M.D. and D.Van Gelden Kurtz, Quest Books, 1997

Chakra Workout, Barka and Jones, Llewellan Publications, St. Paul, MN, 1996

The Chakras, CW Leadbeater, Quest Books-Theosophical Publications (original 1927), 1997

3. For more information on mental toughness see:

The New Toughness Training for Sports, James E. Lohrer, PLUME-Penguin, New York, London, 1995

4. Other books in the Ultimate Training Series from VeloPress include:

The Female Cyclist, Gale Bernhardt, 1999

Complete Guide to Sports Nutrition, Monique Ryan, 1999

Off-Season Training for Cyclists, Edmund R. Burke

Weight Training for Cyclists, Eric Schmitz and Ken Doyle, 1998

5. Other books by Dr. Saul Miller:

Performing Under Pressure, McGraw Hill Ryerson, Toronto, 1992

A Little Relaxation, Hartley & Marks, Vancouver, 1993

Food For Thought: A New Look at Food and Behavior, Prentice Hall, Englewood Cliffs, NJ, 1979

ABOUT THE AUTHORS

Dr. Saul Miller is one of North America's leading sport psychologists. His clients have included the New York Mets, the Los Angeles Dodgers, Rams and Kings, the Vancouver Canucks, St. Louis Blues, Florida Panthers and Seattle Mariners, as well as PGA Tour golfers, and U.S. and Canadian national and Olympic athletes in more than a dozen different sports.

Dr. Miller began consulting with Canada's national cycling team in 1983. He has worked with road, track and mountain-bike racers. Over the years, his clients have won medals at many international events including the Olympic Games and world championships.

COURTESY DR. SAUL MILLER

Dr. Miller is the author of three books: *Performing Under Pressure* (McGraw-Hill Ryerson, Toronto, 1992); *A Little Relaxation* (Hartley & Marks, Vancouver, 1991); and *Food For Thought: A New Look at Food and Behavior* (Prentice Hall, Englewood Cliffs, NJ, 1979).

Peggy Maass Hill has been a competitive cyclist for many years. As a bicycle racer, she was renowned for her diversity. At the 1985 world championships, Maass Hill was a bronze

medalist in individual pursuit. In the 1988 world championships, she was eighth in the points race, and in the 1989 world championships, she was fifth in team time trial. Maass Hill won the 1986 U.S. national criterium title, and the 1988 kilometer title. She still holds the ultra marathon world record—490.5 miles in 24 hours (human-paced). For the past nine years, she has been coaching cyclists in Vancouver, British Columbia. A Level Three Certified Coach, she has been both a provincial and Canadian National Team coach, and is a founder of the Krebs Cycle Club.

ULTIMATE TRAINING SERIES

Complete Guide to Sports Nutrition
By Monique Ryan

Monique Ryan has been the nutrition consultant to the Saturn Cycling Team, the Volvo-Cannondale mountain bike racing team, and many others in her 13 years as an expert in sports nutrition. Her new book is a wealth of cutting-edge information and concepts explained clearly. No other sports nutrition book places such a needed emphasis on menu and meal planning, food strategies, weight management, and other practical food-related topics.
336 pp • Charts, graphs and tables • Paperback
P-NUT $16.95

The Female Cyclist: Gearing Up a Level
by Gale Bernhardt

Perfect for the woman cyclist who enjoys cycling for fitness and wants to improve her riding skills and achieve higher goals. Includes special chapter on bike fit, as well as detailed programs for blending cycling and training, women's health and nutrition, and tips for making cycling more comfortable. Great information for male cyclists, too!
6" x 9" • 352 pp • Paperback
P-FEM $16.95

Off-Season Training for Cyclists
by Edmund R. Burke, Ph.D.

Get a jump on the competition with this VeloPress Ultimate Training Series book from Ed Burke. Burke takes you through everything you need to know about winter training — indoor workouts, weight training, cross-training, periodization and more. The best cyclists in the world are doing it; you can't afford not to.
6" x 9" • 200 pp • Paperback
P-OFF $14.95

Weight Training for Cyclists
by Eric Schmitz and Ken Doyle

Written from the premise that optimum cycling performance demands total body strength, this book informs the serious cyclist on how to increase strength with weight training, as cycling alone cannot completely develop the muscle groups used while riding.
6" x 9" • 200 pp • Paperback
P-WTC $14.95

TO ORDER, CALL 800/234-8356
OR VISIT US ON THE WEB AT WWW.VELOGEAR.COM